DARING THE UNKNOWN

Howard E. Smith

DARING THE UNKNOWN

A HISTORY OF NASA

GULLIVER BOOKS
HARCOURT BRACE JOVANOVICH
San Diego   Austin   Orlando

Photographs compliments of the National Aeronautics and
Space Administration

Library of Congress Cataloging-in-Publication Data
Smith, Howard Everett, 1927–
    Daring the unknown.
    "Gulliver books."
    Bibliography: p.
    Includes index.
    Summary: A chronicle of the technological and
political challenges, the people, and the discoveries
of the American space program during the last thirty
years.
    1. National Aeronautics and Space Administration—
History—Juvenile literature. [1. National Aeronautics
and Space Administration—History] I. Title.
TL793.S586 1987   353.0087′78   86-33617
ISBN 0-15-200435-1

Designed by Dalia Hartman
Printed in the United States of America

First edition

A B C D E

To Adam and Aaron, who will witness wonders in the sky

Contents

Black-and-White Photographs

Color Photographs

DARING THE UNKNOWN

1

The Dawn of the Space Age

Who has not looked at the night sky and wondered what was out there in space? Far away in the vast universe are stars, planets, and moons waiting to be explored. Strange and exciting adventures might lie in store for us, or riches beyond belief. Perhaps even life—maybe lowly plants like seaweeds, or huge dinosaurlike animals. Maybe beings as intelligent as we are—or more intelligent.

Human beings are explorers at heart. We have gone everywhere we could, from the North and South Poles to the source of the Nile River, from hidden depths of the ocean to the highest mountains. Now in this, the "Space Age," we are moving for the first time ever out into space itself—out to the moon, toward the planets, and someday, no doubt, to the stars. We have never stopped exploring and we never will. Although exploring is a risky business, we must do it because we are human beings. To be human is to seek.

Today we stand on our little planet Earth (so very small compared to many planets) and look up at the sky. We stand at the edge of the space that surrounds us—a space so vast, so distant that we have no idea how far it extends.

The age of space exploration has begun. We can date the beginning of the Space Age from October 4, 1957, when the Soviet Union launched the first artificial satellite, which they named *Sputnik*.

But the Space Age did not start that suddenly. The groundwork for it began many centuries ago, with the invention of skyrockets.

THE EARLIEST ROCKETS

No one really knows when the first skyrocket streaked into the air, but we do know where. An unknown Chinese inventor (probably during the thirteenth century) put gunpowder into a tube that was closed at one end and open at the other. He lit it and watched it rise into the air and explode like fireworks. That was a rocket.

At first rockets were probably toys used mostly for entertainment and celebrations. Later, Chinese troops fired rockets at their enemies. Some were fired at invaders from the top of the Great Wall of China.

For centuries, no one really knew why or how rockets worked.

Isaac Newton, a British scientist who lived from 1642 to 1727, studied the laws of motion. He stated that for every action there is an equal and opposite reaction. What does this mean? If you fill up a balloon with air and then release it, the air will rush out of the balloon and the balloon will shoot off in the opposite direction. The air coming out of the balloon is the "action," and the motion of the balloon is the "reaction."

This law, called Newton's Third Law of Motion, explains how rockets move. The flames coming out of a rocket are the action. The forward motion of the rocket is the reaction.

After Newton's time, rockets continued to be used

mostly for entertainment such as fireworks and, on occasion, in warfare. (We know from "The Star-Spangled Banner" with its phrase "by the rocket's red glare" that rockets were used in the War of 1812.)

Though every child in centuries past probably wondered how high rockets could go, and may have dreamed of sending a rocket all the way to the moon, no one took such ideas seriously. But in the late nineteenth century, things changed. There was a surge of interest in science and technology. New ideas and new dreams stimulated people.

One who dreamed of space travel and rockets was Konstantin Eduardovitch Tsiolkovsky.

OF SPACE AND TSIOLKOVSKY

Tsiolkovsky was born on September 17, 1857, in the small Russian town of Izhevskoye. He lost his hearing at age nine, and four years later his mother died. As a result, he grew to be a shy and often lonely person. However, Tsiolkovsky was very good at mathematics and physics, and he put most of his efforts into his studies.

When he was nineteen, Tsiolkovsky began to teach school in Borovsk. In his free time he worked on his own ideas, including the writing of a paper on the kinetic theory of gases. In 1892 he designed and built the first wind tunnel in Russia and used it to test dirigible (lighter-than-air aircraft) designs. The Academy of Sciences gave him a grant. With a larger and better wind tunnel he tested numerous aircraft to see how the friction of air would affect them.

In 1895 Tsiolkovsky published the book for which he is best known today, *Dreams of Earth and Space*. The following year he began his most interesting and serious work, *Exploration of Cosmic Space by Means of Reaction Devices*.

The "reaction devices" were, of course, rockets and rocket engines. In this work he also wrote about advanced navigational equipment that space travelers could use, proposed fuel supplies, and described how the friction of air on rockets leaving and entering the atmosphere would produce immense heat.

Although Tsiolkovsky did few experiments aside from those in his wind tunnel, and none with rockets (nor did he ever build an actual rocket), he single-handedly started the science of space travel. Even before the first airplane flew, he saw and understood most of the major problems of travel with rockets. His writings paved a way to the understanding of space travel.

What was needed to carry forward Tsiolkovsky's work was for someone actually to build a rocket that could go much higher than the ones that had been used for centuries. If space travel was ever to become a reality, someone had to build a new type of rocket—one much more powerful.

OF ROCKETS AND GODDARD

In the late nineteenth and early twentieth centuries, few Americans had heard of Tsiolkovsky. Space travel was still for dreamers and science fiction writers. But one man helped make the dream of space travel a reality. Robert Goddard, born in Massachusetts on October 5, 1882, would go down in history with Tsiolkovsky as one of the founding fathers of the Space Age.

A bright young lad, who learned to repair machines in his father's machine shop, Goddard had no idea what he wanted to do in life. Then he read H. G. Wells's famous book *The War of the Worlds*, a novel that describes how Martians come to Earth in spacecrafts and threaten to take over our planet. The book inflamed Goddard's imagination, and in 1899, sitting in a back yard cherry tree, he decided that he would make a device that had, as he said, "the possibility of going to Mars." Always a good student, Robert

Dr. Robert Goddard stands next to one of his rockets in his Roswell, New Mexico, workshop in October 1935. Goddard was the first man to build and launch a liquid fuel rocket.

Goddard studied mathematics and physics. He received a Ph.D. from Clark University, and went on to teach physics there. When he was not teaching classes he devoted his time to studying and testing rockets.

Goddard's first experimental rockets were of a completely different design and more powerful than any that had been made before. In addition, he proved beyond any doubt that a rocket could move in a vacuum. Next, Goddard turned his attention to fuel.

Tsiolkovsky had written that a rocket capable of going to the moon must be powered by liquid fuels, and that the best combination would be kerosene and liquid oxygen. (This combination was used in 1969 by the *Saturn 5* rocket that lifted men to the moon.) Goddard, who did not know of Tsiolkovsky's work, came to the same conclusion. But unlike Tsiolkovsky, Goddard was a skilled machinist capable of making a liquid-fueled rocket.

On March 16, 1926, Goddard took his first liquid-fueled rocket to his Aunt Effie's farm near Auburn, Massachusetts. Fueled with liquid oxygen and gasoline, it flew for two and a half seconds and rose to a height of 41 feet. The first liquid-fueled rocket ever to rise from the ground, it opened the door to the Space Age.

The famous aviator Charles Lindbergh learned about Goddard's work and gave him funds so that he could do more research. With the money Goddard went to Roswell, New Mexico, where there was enough open space for him to launch more rockets without making his neighbors nervous.

In New Mexico, one of Goddard's rockets reached a height of one mile above the ground and moved so fast it broke the sound barrier. No airplane in the world had ever exceeded the speed of sound.

Goddard not only made the first liquid-fueled rockets, but he also made the first fuel pumps for them and invented steering devices that could guide them.

Robert Goddard's work was so well done that rockets have changed very little since his time. Even the largest and most complex rockets of today are basically the same as those that Robert Goddard made and flew in New Mexico.

THE GERMAN SOCIETY FOR SPACE TRAVEL

It is truly amazing that so few knew of the work of Tsiolkovsky and Goddard. Most scientists ignored space travel and rockets as dreams and ideas of no importance. Even so, change was in the air.

In 1927 in Germany, a group of men would get together and begin thinking about space travel and rockets. The society they would form, called the German Society for Space Travel, would have an immense impact on the future of the world.

Many members of the German Society for Space Travel became famous, among them Hermann Julius Oberth, Wernher von Braun, and Willy Ley, a famous popularizer of space travel.

Wernher von Braun

Of all the members of the German Society for Space Travel, Wernher von Braun was destined to become the most famous. More than the others, he would guide the world into the Space Age.

Wernher von Braun was born March 23, 1912, in Wirsitz, Germany. His family were landowners, and his father was a baron.

From an early age von Braun was a brilliant student who loved mathematics and science. When he was 18 years old, he read an article on space travel and the exploration of the moon. He decided then to spend his life studying, building, and understanding rockets.

He studied engineering at the technological institutes of Berlin and of Zurich, Switzerland, where he met Professor Hermann Oberth. In the summer of 1930, he, Oberth, and others used a vacant lot to test rockets they had made. By the time von Braun received his B.S. degree in engineering, in June 1932, he had helped launch more than 85 rockets. He had also read some of the writings of Robert Goddard, who was far better known in Europe and especially Germany than in his own country.

In 1932 some German army officers watched a rocket launching. Impressed, they asked von Braun and the others to work for the German army. Von Braun said they did not want to build weapons nor did they care about the army. But because they needed the money, they agreed.

Von Braun was made the chief of the experiment station at Kummersdorf and was called the "wonder boy" because he was so young. In 1934, at the age of twenty-one, he earned his Ph.D. degree.

When Hitler rose to power in 1933, he became interested in the rockets and financed more research. At the research center at Peenemunde on the Baltic Sea, von Braun and his associates designed and built powerful engines, pumps, and steering fins. They also produced gyroscopes that would keep the rockets stable in flight. By 1936 von Braun had designed a prototype rocket, the original design for a V2 rocket. It could travel eleven miles, a far greater distance than any rocket had ever gone.

During the early part of World War II, Hitler's armies were winning battles without rockets, and he lost interest in them. With limited funds, von Braun continued to make improvements on the V2. On October 3, 1942, the improved V2 was fired. It weighed 28,000 pounds and was 46 feet high and 65 inches in diameter—by far the largest rocket ever made. It could be launched from an easily built platform of only 25 square feet, carry a ton of explosives, and fly a distance of 190 miles.

Now Hitler was interested once more. No other aircraft in the world, aside from an airplane, could reach a distance of 190 miles. And the rocket traveled too fast to be shot down. The Germans pushed the production of the new V2's. To hasten things, they used Eastern European prisoners captured during the war to work on the rockets.

On September 6, 1944, a V2 was aimed toward England and fired. The Germans had no idea where it would really land, although they hoped it would hit London.

The V2 hit a main railroad station and blew it to pieces, killing many Londoners. The British government was stunned and thought the Germans had a new weapon that was not only fast and powerful, but terribly accurate as well.

Eventually, thousands of rockets were fired toward English cities. Before the war was over, von Braun and his associates were studying ways to make a rocket that could reach New York City.

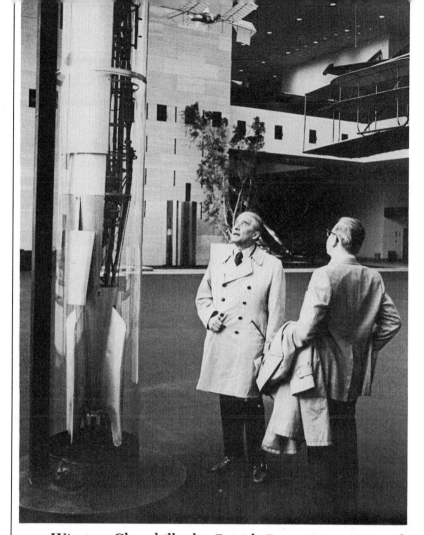

Dr. Wernher von Braun, the father of modern rocketry.

Winston Churchill, the British Prime Minister, said after the war was over that if the Germans had made the V2 rocket a few years earlier, England would have been forced to surrender. Germany would have won the war.

In spite of the V2's, the war was coming to an end for the Germans. Von Braun and his brother Magnus surrendered to American troops in 1945. American officers and interviewers did not believe that von Braun had invented the V2: He seemed much too young, too fat, and too jovial.

When American and British scientists spoke with him at first, they, too, were puzzled by his youth and good humor. But when they asked him technical engineering

9

and scientific questions, they quickly learned that they were speaking to one of the most remarkable engineers of the twentieth century.

Persuaded by American army officials, von Braun signed a one-year contract, which he later renewed, to come to the United States and work for the army. Willy Ley and others also moved to the United States. Von Braun was sent to Fort Bliss, Texas, where he led the first American research on the new powerful rockets. Under his direction, the United States made swift progress in rocket research.

Using the V2 as a model, von Braun designed the *Redstone* rocket, which would later be used to put the first Americans into space on suborbital trips. By 1960, now a U.S. citizen, he headed the George C. Marshall Space Flight Center in Huntsville, Alabama. He designed the powerful *Saturn* rockets, which were later used by NASA to put men on the moon.

After the war, not much work besides von Braun's was done on rockets in the United States, England, or other countries in Western Europe. Almost all scientists and engineers were working on other projects. Rockets were almost completely forgotten in America. So was space travel. No one would have believed that before a generation had passed, a rocket would take men to the moon.

2

Sputnik: The Space Age Begins

THE FIRST DAYS OF THE SPACE AGE

Meanwhile, the Soviet Union, we now know, was secretly speeding up all of its rocket research. The Soviets were particularly interested in building large, powerful rockets. A rocket of sufficient size and power, they realized, might manage to get a tiny object into orbit.

On October 4, 1957, the world was amazed to learn that the Russians had launched a satellite called *Sputnik* into orbit around the earth. Every 96 minutes, the tiny satellite circled the world from a height of between 142 and 588 miles. *Sputnik* was a sphere only 23 inches across, and it weighed a little over 184 pounds. Attached to it were four antennae, each between eight and nine and a half feet long. A thermometer on board registered the temperature of space around the satellite, and a radio sent information about the temperature to Earth.

The world was shocked. At the time, only a few scientists realized that a man-made object could orbit the earth. So strange was the idea that most people were baffled, and some frightened. Almost everyone wanted to know more about this thrilling, miraculous achievement. Newspapers everywhere had to explain what an orbit was, define the term satellite, and inform readers about weightlessness.

What Is an Orbit?

What makes a satellite—*Sputnik* or any other satellite (the moon included)—orbit the earth? That is, why will something go around and around the earth and stay at the same height above the earth, day after day, year after year, even for hundreds of millions of years?

Imagine that someone is standing on top of a very high tower, far above the earth's atmosphere. Say she has a cannon up there and several cannonballs.

If she drops a cannonball it will fall to the foot of the tower. If, however, she puts a cannonball into the cannon and fires it, the cannonball will go for a long distance from the tower (perhaps a few miles) before it falls to the ground. If the cannon is very powerful, the cannonball might go twenty, thirty, forty miles or more before it hits the ground. And if the cannon were truly remarkable, it might be able to shoot the cannonball all the way around the world. If so, that cannonball will never reach the ground. It will go around the world and go right by the tower. Again and again it could circle the world and never stop. The cannonball would be in orbit.

Then what happens? First of all, the cannonball keeps falling. The earth's gravity keeps pulling it downward. At first you'd think the cannonball would hit the ground. But if it's going fast enough, it won't. Why? The earth is round. When an orbiting cannonball falls, it never hits the ground because the curve of the earth's surface moves downward under it just as fast as the cannonball falls. It can never catch up with the "falling" surface of the earth below it.

What Is Weightlessness?

A satellite in orbit is "weightless." Anyone in a satellite

would also be weightless. So would objects in the satellite—books, tools, food, drops of water, or anything else.

As we just saw, a satellite in orbit around the earth keeps falling toward the earth. Not only does the satellite constantly fall, but so does everything inside of it.

Now pretend that someone has placed a box in an elevator that's being monitored by a television camera. Let us say that the box weighs 100 pounds and that it is resting on a scale. If the elevator is not moving, the scale will read 100 pounds. If the elevator starts moving downward, the weight of the box, according to the scale, will be less. If the elevator cable breaks and the elevator falls, the box also falls, though, of course, it stays in the elevator. The camera, focused on the scale, will record a weight of zero. The box weighs nothing.

Until the cable broke, it supported the elevator. Gravity pulled down on the box, and its weight pushed downward against the scale. But when the cable broke, the elevator and the scale on the floor fell, moving downward at the same speed as the box fell. The box no longer pushed against the scale, so it showed the box as weighing zero, or, in other words, as being weightless.

Anyone in an orbiting spacecraft will *apparently* be weightless, for the floor of the spacecraft is falling away from him or her as fast as he or she is falling. That person, like the box, would not be able to press against a scale so that it registered any weight at all.

Anything that is loose inside a satellite is also falling toward the earth. The objects inside fall at the same rate of speed.

THE CHALLENGE OF *SPUTNIK*

Sputnik was a glorious triumph for the Soviet Union. It had a tremendous impact upon Americans, who had prided themselves on their leadership in the world of science.

Many in the United States were stunned that a country they considered backward could have invented the first satellite and put it into space. Educators worried that schools were not doing a good job of teaching science. After *Sputnik* went up, American schools placed much greater emphasis on science courses for children.

Most people in the U.S. government and military were also concerned. The military saw in *Sputnik* a threat to the United States. If the Russians could get *Sputnik* up, they might be able to send an atomic or hydrogen bomb anywhere in the country.

Then, less than a month later, the Soviet Union again surprised the world. On November 3, 1957, they sent up *Sputnik 2*. (The original *Sputnik* became known as *Sputnik 1*.) At 1,121 pounds, *Sputnik 2* was much larger than *Sputnik 1*. Built in the form of a steel cylinder, it carried a dog named Laika. Instruments recorded the dog's heartbeats and other information to determine if a mammal could live in space. After ten days in space, *Sputnik*'s oxygen supply ended and Laika died. Laika proved that at least for several days a mammal could survive in space.

PRESIDENT DWIGHT D. EISENHOWER AND NASA

When Dwight D. Eisenhower became president of the United States in January 1953 the Space Age was hardly a dream, even for most scientists and military officials.

When the first *Sputnik* went up, Eisenhower was in his second term as president. Everyone wondered what his response would be. To the surprise of most people, he played it down. At a press conference he said, "[*Sputnik*] does not raise my apprehension one iota." He did not believe that it gained the Soviet Union any degree of military power. Moreover, he had great confidence in America's space efforts, as modest as they were.

Eisenhower's aides took up his views. One called *Sput-*

nik a "silly bauble." Another said that *Sputnik* would be forgotten in six months.

During the months after *Sputnik* went up, Eisenhower and his close advisers remained unflappable. In public they refused to treat it as an important event. To do so would have made America's military might appear weakened, they felt. Moreover, they did not want to call attention to the fact that American space efforts, funded by the government, had achieved few successes and none which could be called dramatic during the Eisenhower administration.

But most Americans felt deep concern. *Sputnik*, they believed, called for a swift and dramatic response. Many were not pleased with Eisenhower's attempts to minimize an event that was obviously a scientific breakthrough.

Newspapers and magazines tended to reflect the majority view. The magazine *Commonweal*, for example, said, "Those few who scoff at the importance of the earth satellite, including the president himself, failed to convince anyone."

Following *Sputnik*, Eisenhower's popularity with the public declined, according to polls. Whether or not this decline was caused by his position on *Sputnik* is hard to tell. He had suffered a heart attack, the USSR had rebuffed him at a summit meeting, and the economy was down. His attempts to ignore the relevance of *Sputnik* no doubt added to his political decline.

In spite of all, Eisenhower continued to downplay *Sputnik*. His policy toward space was probably most clearly spelled out by his science adviser, James Killian, in a speech given on December 13, 1960. Killian pointed out that the Soviet achievements in space were used for propaganda purposes. In the long run, he said, such efforts would not sustain an image of strength. If the United States copied Soviet space accomplishments, he continued, it would admit to being second best and thus lower the country's international prestige.

He also mentioned the costs. He said that while the

space program and man-in-space program satisfied the administration and were needed, they must be contained. Otherwise the United States would be faced with a multi-billion-dollar space program. Would such expenditures in space pay off, he asked, as well as an additional several billion dollars a year for quality education? Many critics of the space program would agree, even today, with Killian's remarks. But there were a majority of those who did not.

SENATOR JOHNSON ESTABLISHES AMERICA'S SPACE PROGRAM

While Eisenhower was president, the second most influential politician in the United States was Senator Lyndon B. Johnson of Texas, who held the powerful position of Senate majority leader. Johnson was a Democrat, and often had views opposite to Eisenhower, a Republican.

On the first night that *Sputnik* circled the earth, Johnson was at his ranch in Texas. He went outside and watched the pinpoint of light that was *Sputnik* moving across the vast Texas sky. Until then he had always considered the skies of Texas to be friendly, he said. But as he watched, he had some doubts. He said he also realized "that America was not ahead in everything."

Senator Johnson spent most of the rest of that night on the telephone, talking with powerful political figures all over the United States, getting the pulse of the country's feeling about *Sputnik*. He came to realize that *Sputnik* was an event of great importance, especially to America's foreign policy. Even if it were not a major military threat, it had to have serious consequences. Johnson wondered how America would be seen by other countries. He decided that he himself would take a major leadership role in the coming Space Age.

Johnson took immediate steps. On the opening day of

the 1958 session of Congress, Senator Johnson, breaking with tradition, gave a "private State of the Union" address of his own to Congress. The central task of the forthcoming session, he stressed, was to form an organization and program that would ensure American superiority in space. The Congress, already behind Johnson, was impressed.

This speech obviously went directly counter to the views of the Eisenhower administration. Congress, under the leadership of Johnson and despite the president's efforts to the contrary, would do all it could to bring the United States into a space race.

3

NASA: The Challenge

THE FOUNDING OF NASA

Next, Senator Johnson set up the Preparedness Subcommittee to investigate America's space needs. Lengthy hearings showed that the research and development programs in existence were inadequate and poorly coordinated. At that time, America's space efforts were scattershot, carried out by the Air Force, the Army, the Navy, the National Advisory Committee on Aeronautics (NACA), universities, and other organizations. No specific goals had been set forth. Worse, agencies often had no idea what advances other agencies were making. A single centralized space agency with full responsibility for civilian aeronautical and space research was clearly needed.

At the end of the congressional hearings, only one question remained: Should the space agency be run by the military or by civilians? Congress took a vote, and there was strong backing for a civilian agency.

On February 10, 1958, the Senate set up a special committee to review the matter. And on March 5 the House of Representatives set up their special committee. Pressure from the Congress (and the public) forced Eisenhower to act. On April 12 he recommended that all space activities "except those projects primarily associated with military requirements" be conducted by a new National Aeronautics and Space Administration. NASA, as it would be called, was to succeed the older NACA.

By July, both the Senate and the House had passed bills to establish NASA. As finally enacted and signed into law by Eisenhower, the National Aeronautics and Space Act of 1958 declared that U.S. policy would be "devoted to peaceful purposes for the benefit of all mankind," and left the responsibility for the formulation of NASA policy up to the president. Thus, NASA was established on October 1, 1958.

The Act also made the president responsible for developing a "comprehensive program" of space activities. It was up to him to assign military applications to the Defense Department, and to resolve disputes between agencies. The president would obtain the advice of a nine-member National Aeronautics and Space Council, which he would head. NASA would be headed by a civilian administrator. An appropriation of $80 million was given to NASA for 1959.

On August 15 President Eisenhower's nomination of T. Keith Glennan as NASA's first administrator was confirmed by Congress. Glennan had been president of Case Institute of Technology. His appointment was confirmed August 19.

The government had established NASA and now found itself firmly in the Space Age. To oversee the American commitment to the new age, the House, on July 21, set up a 25-member Committee on Science and Astronautics. On July 24 the Senate set up its own 15-member Aeronautical and Space Science Committee.

NASA'S ORGANIZATION

Under Glennan's direction, NASA set to work coordinating its many activities, centers, and employees. Working under

Glennan was the new deputy director, Hugh L. Dryden, who had been the highly respected director of NACA. At Langley Research Center in Hampton, Virginia, Director Robert Gilruth became chief of a special task force to develop a manned satellite program.

Langley, established in 1917, was one of the oldest but most up-to-date aeronautical facilities in America. Since its founding, research had focused on aircraft development. In 1958, when NASA took over and Gilruth became chief, the focus of research shifted to a manned capsule. The future *Mercury*, *Gemini*, and *Apollo* spacecraft were all to be developed at Langley.

At the Marshall Space Flight Center in Huntsville, Alabama, workers under the direction of Wernher von Braun had built the U.S. Army *Redstone* rocket. Beginning in 1958, under NASA's direction, von Braun headed a team that would build the famous *Saturn* family of rockets. Eventually a *Saturn* rocket would propel men to the moon. Skylab, the first space station, would also be developed there, along with lunar rovers and the engines for the space shuttle.

Abe Silverstein, director of the Lewis Research Center, NACA's old propulsion laboratory in Cleveland, Ohio, became director of NASA's spaceflight programs. At Lewis, Silverstein took over the successful development of the *Centaur* rocket, which would take *Surveyor I* to the moon for a lunar landing. The *Agenda* rocket, which would propel *Ranger* spacecraft to the moon for photographic maps of its surface, would also be developed there.

By the time NASA was established, NACA engineers working with engineer H. Julian Allen at the Ames Aeronautical Laboratory in Moffett Field near San Francisco, California, had already discovered that the best shape for a spacecraft entering the earth's atmosphere was blunt-nosed. This shape would be used both by American and by Soviet spacecraft. Under NASA, Ames continued valuable aeronautic research and later conducted studies of the effects of space travel on humans.

The Goddard Space Flight Center in Greenbelt, Maryland, was to be responsible for over half the American satellites launched into space. It would also become the headquarters of STADAN, the worldwide Space Tracking and Data Acquisition Network for tracking unmanned satellites.

The Jet Propulsion Laboratory (JPL) predated the founding of NASA by many years. In 1944 the U.S. Army set it up for missile development. Its staff and operation were directed by the prestigious California Institute of Technology. Since NASA took over JPL, there has been some friction between the two organizations, because JPL has always considered itself to be at least partly independent of direct NASA authority.

Before and after it became connected with NASA, JPL was directed by a New Zealand–born physicist, William H. Pickering. Very shortly after NASA was founded, Abe Silverstein of the Lewis Research Center asked Pickering to study a spacecraft that would take and send a great number of photographic images of the moon. Pickering and others at JPL developed the *Ranger* spacecraft, destined to be the first true spacecraft. It was the first ever to incorporate a system that would navigate in reference to the sun, the earth, and a chosen star; the first to carry a solar-powered system; the first to be able to make its own flight corrections in midcourse; and the first to use a two-step launch. It was designed to carry cameras to photograph the moon's surface and a communication system to radio the information back to JPL receivers. Many say that with the *Ranger*, the United States began interplanetary exploration.

JPL was also to develop the highly successful *Explorer* (America's first satellite), the *Mariner*, and the *Viking* spacecraft.

At Edwards Air Force Base in California (later to be

named the Hugh L. Dryden Flight Center after the former NACA director and NASA's first deputy administrator), preparations were begun for the recruitment and training of NASA's first astronauts, many of whom would be found among the test pilots at Edwards.

In 1961 NASA set up the Houston Manned Space Center near Clear Lake, Texas, southeast of Houston. The center houses Mission Control, which directs manned space missions after lift-off. In 1965 *Gemini 4* was the first such mission. In 1973 the center was renamed the Johnson Space Center in honor of President Lyndon B. Johnson, who did so much to help found and support NASA. In addition to controlling manned missions in space, the center is responsible for the design and management of spacecraft as well as for astronaut selection and training. Also found at the center is the Lunar Receiving Laboratory, where moon rocks are stored and studied, and the Lunar Scientific Institute, which Rice University operates there.

NASA also acquired responsibility for Cape Canaveral, where almost every famous rocket launch was to take place; Michoud Assembly Facility at Michoud, Louisiana; Flight Research Center at Murdoc, California; and the Wallops Island, Virginia, substation of Langley Research Center. NASA set up an operating agreement with the U.S. Army, which controls White Sands, to carry out more rocket experiments there.

All NASA employees and centers are under the direction of NASA headquarters, located in Washington, D.C.

In a few years, NASA grew into an immense organization. Its budget nearly doubled each year until it reached an all-time peak of $5.25 billion in 1965. In 1966 its staff also peaked. At that time 34,000 people worked directly for NASA, and another 400,000 employees worked on agency programs.

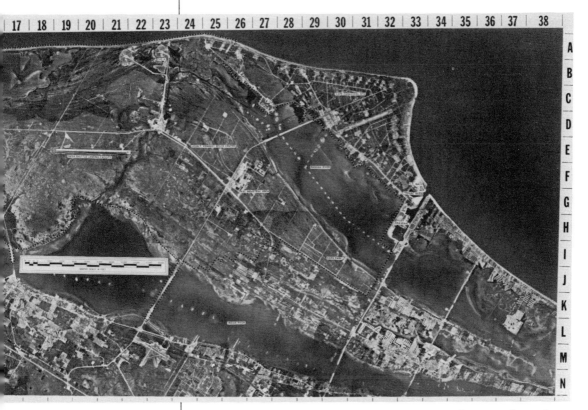

A
B
C
D
E
F
G
H
I
J
K
L
M
N

Cape Canaveral, as seen from a height of 18,000 feet.

T. Keith Glennan's administration of NASA lasted until January 20, 1961, when he was succeeded by James E. Webb, who held the post from February 14, 1961, to October 7, 1968, longer than any NASA administrator. Following Webb, Thomas O. Paine was appointed administrator on March 21, 1969, and held the post until September 15, 1970; James C. Fletcher took over on April 27, 1971, and remained until May 1, 1977; Robert A. Frosch took over on June 21, 1977, and held the post until January 20, 1981; and James Beggs took over on July 10, 1981, remaining until December 4, 1985. On May 12, 1986, James C. Fletcher once again became NASA's administrator and holds the post as of this printing.

With these leaders and the many thousands of men and women who worked at the various centers, NASA undertook the journey that would see the manned exploration of the moon and send spacecraft to the distant planets, with some going onward toward the stars themselves. The great adventure had begun.

NASA'S INHERITANCE

America's space efforts before NASA hardly made for a rousing success story, but each proved useful to NASA's future endeavors.

By December 1957, the U.S. Navy had a rocket ready to launch—a mere two months after *Sputnik 1* went into orbit. It was named *Vanguard 1*. The rocket was placed on a launchpad and prepared for a flight that would take it and a small satellite into orbit around the earth. A huge crowd gathered at Cape Canaveral to watch the launch, to prove to the world that the United States could do anything in space as well as the Soviet Union. Television cameras prepared to record the historic moment.

Just after the countdown took place, flames spewed out from under the rocket. The *Vanguard* began to move. A second later the rocket stalled a few feet above the ground, hovered in the air, then fell backward and crashed onto the launchpad. As it exploded, an enormous ball of flame hid the rocket from sight.

Then an odd thing happened. Just as the rocket exploded, it released the satellite. It shot several feet up into the air, headed back down, hit the ground, and rolled across a field. As it did, its radio went, "Beep, beep, beep."

Along with the *Vanguard* workers, Americans felt sick. Over the next weeks engineers redesigned many parts of the rocket and made many changes. Another *Vanguard 1* rocket stood on the launchpad on February 5, 1958, ready once more to send a satellite into space. That rocket also failed. Between December 1957 and September 1958, U.S. Navy *Vanguard* rockets and their satellites failed many times.

Each failure, however, taught scientists something new and important about rocket and engine designs, the design of radios, and much more. Developments in other fields, especially in computer technology, were also moving ahead at full speed.

While the *Vanguard* rockets provided little cause for celebration, other scientists tasted success with the *Juno* rocket. On January 31, 1958, a U.S. Army *Juno 1* rocket stood on a launchpad at Cape Canaveral. The countdown was given. Everyone watched with fingers crossed as *Juno 1* moved ever so slowly upward, heading for the sky. Five minutes after lift-off, it released a small satellite called *Explorer*.

A model of *Explorer I*, the first satellite that the United States placed in orbit. The eighteen-pound *Explorer I* was launched by a *Jupiter C* rocket on January 31, 1958. It discovered the Van Allen radiation belt, which surrounds the earth.

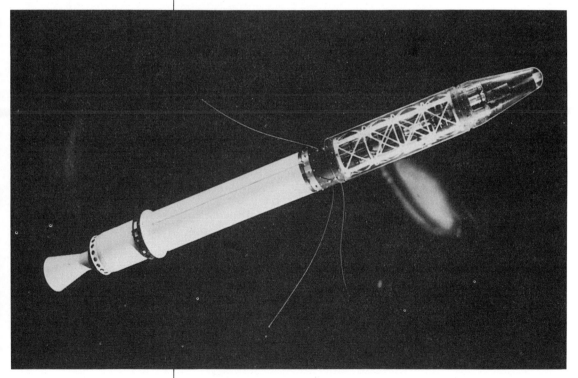

The *Explorer* satellite was not a dramatic-looking piece of equipment. It was a mere 40 inches long and only six inches in diameter. It weighed only 10.5 pounds. Even so, it would make history.

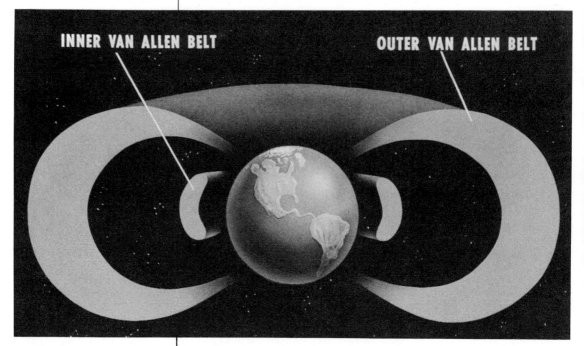

INNER VAN ALLEN BELT   OUTER VAN ALLEN BELT

A diagram of the Van Allen radiation belt.

The *Explorer* circled the earth in an unusual orbit. At its lowest it came within 224 miles of the earth's surface, and at its highest it was 1,575 miles above the earth. As it continuously circled the globe, it constantly shifted its orbit so that it explored a huge sphere of space surrounding the earth.

Constant radio signals let scientists know that the earth is surrounded by a huge doughnut-shaped field of radioactive particles. This region was named the Van Allen belt, after James Van Allen, the scientist who thought up the experiments and put into the satellite the Geiger counters that measured the radioactivity.

Nikita Khrushchev, the Russian premier, called the *Explorer* nothing more than a grapefruit. He laughed in public, but Russian scientists were taken by surprise by the size of the instruments the satellite carried. The tiny radio, in particular, puzzled them, for they could not make one so small, nor such small instruments. These miniature satellites, they realized, could do as much as their large sat-

26

ellites. And if the United States were to send up a big satellite, it could be filled with hundreds, even thousands of instruments.

THE EARLY DAYS OF NASA

NASA's first days posed a unique challenge. Rarely in history has there been such a coordinated effort of politicians, administrators, and world-famous scientists to take on so many unknowns. Everything they did would be experimental. As they prepared to explore space with new equipment, they were faced with a huge task and countless difficulties.

With the United States success of *Explorer*, NASA's immediate goal was the further development of American satellites. Rocket improvements were necessary so that satellites could be lofted into space, and the setting up of worldwide communications centers was called for so that a satellite could be tracked once it was in space.

New and far faster computers had to be designed and manufactured for highly specialized tasks. Lightweight materials, especially metals, had to be made for rockets, computers, and onboard equipment. Highly specialized instruments had to be designed to test the environment of space: its temperature, radioactivity, ionization, and other physical characteristics. Cameras, infrared sensors, and much more had to be developed.

Meanwhile, the Soviet Union was advancing on another front. Both their rockets and their satellites were much larger than those of the United States, and the Russians had medical records from dogs they'd sent into space. It was clear from Russian science journals and CIA reports that the Soviet Union was preparing to send a man aloft and into orbit.

NASA speeded up its preparations to orbit its own man in space. The first step was to find out how animals would survive (Russian information about the dogs was kept secret). NASA decided to send a small squirrel monkey aloft in a rocket.

On December 13, 1958, an Army *Jupiter* rocket lifted off carrying a monkey named "Ol' Reliable." The monkey had been trained to turn certain switches off and on one after the other in correct order. As the rocket moved high above the earth and beyond the earth's atmosphere, Ol' Reliable did as he was trained. His body was covered with numerous sensors that recorded his heartbeat, breathing rate, blood pressure, and other changes in his body. Once in space he did all his tasks successfully.

When the rocket came down, scientists and doctors went to pick up Ol' Reliable at sea. Sadly, the nose cone sank beneath the waves, and the monkey was never found. But Ol' Reliable had proved that an animal, and a not-too-distant cousin of humankind's at that, was able to think and work in space. In addition, the record of his heart rate, blood pressure, and other bodily activities showed that while in space he had suffered no harm.

So, in part, it was a monkey that changed American space history. On the evidence of the monkey's flight, NASA decided that America could safely put a man into orbit. And it would do so with Project Mercury.

4

Project Mercury: Manned Flight

THE MAN-IN-SPACE PROGRAM

Project Mercury, the American program to get a man into space, began in 1944. The National Advisory Committee on Aeronautics (NACA) held a seminar to discuss the new German jet-propelled airplanes and America's response to them. In 1945 Congress appropriated $500,000 for a preliminary study of a rocket airplane. Studies were made, and in October 1947 an experimental rocket airplane, the XS-2, broke the sound barrier over Murdoc Dry Lake in California. It reached a record altitude of 43,000 feet—the edge of space.

Of major concern to the scientists and pilots connected with the program was how men could withstand the massive acceleration, or sudden speeding up, on takeoff; the weightlessness while free-falling; and the massive deacceleration, or slowing down, on returning to the ground. To find out, monkeys and mice were shot in rockets to altitudes of up to 45 miles. The animals survived unharmed, indicating that it was possible that men could also withstand such flights in the future. And in the meantime, the U.S.

Air Force and the Navy began experimenting with a human being's ability to withstand G forces.

What Is a G Force?

When we stand on Earth, the earth's gravity pulls us downward. If a person weighs 120 pounds, we say that the earth pulls her downward with a force of 120 pounds. If the same person stood on the moon, where the moon's gravity is only one-sixth that of the earth, she would weigh only 20 pounds. On planet Jupiter, where the gravity is 2.64 times that of Earth, she would weigh 316.8 pounds. The G force, which is the apparent force of gravity, is one G on Earth; one-sixth G on the moon; and 2.64 G's on Jupiter.

G forces not only register gravity, but they also show up when a person accelerates. If you stand in an elevator that suddenly rises, you will feel heavier. The accelerating elevator pushes against you. If you are in a rocket, which accelerates much more rapidly than an elevator, a G force can be so high that you could become unconscious as blood drains from the brain. If high enough, a G force can kill you.

Anytime a rocket or spacecraft accelerates or deaccelerates, a G force is produced. Since no one knew how many G's people could withstand, the military conducted many experiments to find out.

In the spring of 1958, NACA published a report under the direction of Maxime Faget, a talented design engineer at Langley, which was a blueprint for the forthcoming *Mercury* spacecraft. Within days of the formation of NASA, under approval of Congress and President Eisenhower, the American man-in-space program was renamed Project Mercury.

To get a man into space required a rocket, a space

capsule, radios, computers, and much more. The *Redstone* rockets, developed under Wernher von Braun, would serve Project Mercury well at first. Project Mercury began to design and test the *Mercury* capsule. This was the spacecraft in which astronauts would sit while orbiting the world. The cone-shaped capsule had a total length of nine feet seven inches, and its maximum diameter was six feet two inches. It weighed 1,360 kilograms, about 3,000 pounds. At its blunt end was a heat shield. Retro-rockets, also on the blunt end, could slow the capsule down so it could reenter the earth's atmosphere after orbiting in space. Then a parachute would pop out of the nose, open, and slow down the descent of the capsule.

Inside the capsule, an astronaut would sit on a contoured couch, wearing a simple space suit much like those worn by high-altitude test pilots. In an emergency, he could inflate it. Small gas jets could be fired to change the capsule's position in space.

In addition to designing and testing a space capsule and all the other equipment needed for Project Mercury, NASA planned the facilities they needed, especially those radio stations that could communicate back and forth to the man in space. Tracking stations with radio transmitters and receivers were established in Africa, Australia, Hawaii, Mexico, and elsewhere—as well as on board U.S. ships.

Most important of all, however, was the need to find and train the astronauts.

THE ASTRONAUTS

Most scientists working with NASA believed that the *Mercury* space capsule would contain a human being much the same way a can of sardines contains sardines. The astronaut would simply sit inside the capsule and do nothing. Executives in NASA considered simply looking for volunteers with adventurous spirits. President Eisenhower decided that such choices would give the space program a questionable image, so he ordered NASA to recruit test pilots who were members of the armed forces.

Having heard that NASA had originally considered "daredevils, circus performers, and mountain climbers," the pilots, of course, were not interested. They also knew that a monkey had gone into space—not an act that test pilots, who had been in control of the world's most expensive, powerful, and swift airplanes, were anxious to follow. We must remember that when Mercury was first planned, there were no "glamorous" thoughts of getting men on the moon. Manned spaceflights were considered experiments, and not much more.

NASA Administrator Glennan soon let it be known that future astronauts would be sure of excellent careers if they would join NASA and its Mercury Project. Fast advancements, more pay, and, above all, recognition of many types would be theirs. Within a few short months, 110 qualified test pilots signed up.

To qualify, a potential astronaut had to be a test pilot in the armed services; to have at least 1,500 hours of flight time as a jet pilot; to have graduated from college and test-pilot school; and to be younger than 40 years and shorter than 5 feet 11 inches.

The 110 candidates were put through grueling tests. First there were the interviews, which turned out to be so demanding that the Air Force began training pilots in advance on how to behave. Pilots were told how to dress, how to sit, and how to answer questions without being too long-winded or too brief. No detail was overlooked: The pilots were advised to wear knee-length socks and to make sure that when they stood with hands on hips, their thumbs were to the rear (because it was suggested that women stand with thumbs forward). The lengthy interviews probed the pilots' attitudes, abilities, responses, and skills.

The physical exams were extraordinarily difficult. NASA

had little information about what sorts of stress astronauts would encounter during spaceflights. They had to make sure that the men were physically strong, showed great stamina and endurance, and were able to react quickly and think clearly in high-pressure situations. Some of the tests nearly terrified candidates. In one, warm water was poured into one ear while cool water was poured into the other. This made the eyeballs gyrate. In another, candidates were strapped flat on a table that then popped straight up. This measured the ability of their bodies to take the stress of a shifting center of gravity. Metal cups were placed on their eyeballs to test eyeball pressure. Candidates ran on treadmills until their hearts raced at 180 beats per minute. Painful exploratory steel "snakes" were put into their colons.

Psychiatrists questioned the pilots extensively to see if the men were indifferent, hostile, overly nervous, stressed out, or otherwise mentally unfit. Each candidate was given a blank piece of paper and asked what he saw on it. All received IQ tests (the average score was about 130) and tests to determine their powers for abstract thinking.

Finally, of the original 110 candidates—all well educated, most math and engineering whizzes, and all successful test pilots with years of aeronautical experience—seven were chosen: Alan B. Shepard, Jr., Virgil I. (Gus) Grissom, John H. Glenn, Jr., Malcolm (Scott) Carpenter, Walter M. Schirra, Jr., Leroy (Gordon) Cooper, and Donald K. Slayton.

Now two years of intensive training awaited NASA's seven new astronauts. They took 240 hours of courses in meteorology, aerodynamics, communications, rocket propulsion, medicine, physics of the upper atmosphere, astronomy, guidance and navigation, digital computers, flight mechanics, and especially geology. Geology was emphasized because of scientists' great interest in the geology of the moon.

In addition to course work, the astronauts did extensive outdoor training. They went on geologic field trips to the Grand Canyon, the Hawaiian Island volcanoes, the molten rocks in Nevada (where atomic explosions had taken place), cinder cones at Sunset Crater and Meteorite Crater in Arizona, and many other places with any sort of crater, in preparation for a trip to the crater-pocked moon.

In case of a crash landing, they brushed up on their jungle and desert survival techniques, which most had already learned in armed services training. They were taught to cope with difficult tropical conditions; flight paths would cover territories close to the equator. In the Panama jungle, they learned how to find edible palm trees, hunt and cook iguanas, and call for help (clap if necessary). In the Nevada desert, they were taught how to make tents and clothing from parachute material, how to travel at night, and how to find cool spots (in the cliffs or dry streambeds) for resting. During one survival test, some of the astronauts were attacked by chiggers that burrowed into their skin and stung for weeks.

To enable them to experience weightlessness for a few seconds, they floated in the padded belly of a huge cargo plane while it dropped suddenly in midair. They were strapped into training machines that spun them violently, turned them upside down, and started and stopped abruptly while they tried to navigate. And they learned how to use computers, a vital part of the space program.

With the astronauts selected and in training, and the rockets, space capsules, and other equipment being prepared, the Mercury program was well off the ground and moving quickly toward the first manned flight.

A CHIMP IN SPACE

America's first "astronaut," as it happened, was not a highly trained, well-educated test pilot, but a chimpanzee called Ham. Chimpanzees are very much like humans in many ways. Their hearts, their blood circulation, their reflexes are much like ours. Though not as intelligent as humans, they are far smarter than most other animals. Like humans, they can use their hands (and feet) to turn on switches, push buttons, grasp handles, and so on.

Ham's mission would be to test the equipment and space capsule and to provide information on how the body fared in space. NASA doctors wanted to know exactly what happened to the heart in space, how the circulation of blood changed, how fast or slow one might think. They wanted to test the ability to drink, eat, turn switches on and off, and much more, in space.

On January 31, 1961, a group of reporters gathered at Cape Canaveral. Television cameras were aimed at a *Redstone* rocket. On top of it was a *Mercury* space capsule that

One of the five animals on the *Mercury-Atlas* flights. The chimpanzee is dressed up in his flight suit, ready to be strapped into a pressure-tight container with a window dome (bottom left).

had been designed to hold a single astronaut. On that day a cheerful and very healthy chimpanzee sat strapped in the padded seat inside. Perhaps no chimpanzee in history had ever been checked by doctors as thoroughly as Ham.

Americans everywhere, watching television or sitting beside radios, heard the famous countdown for the first time: "Ten, nine, eight, seven, six, five, four, three, two, one, ignition, lift-off."

Ham's trip took him 40 miles higher than planned, to a height of 155 miles above the earth's surface. He traveled 420 miles away from Cape Canaveral.

While he was on that short (17-minute) trip, scientists watched radio-sent recordings of his heart, blood pressure, arm movements, breathing rate, and much more. The recordings also showed Ham correctly turning on and off the switches as he had been trained to do. NASA scientists watched the intelligent chimpanzee and pronounced his performance A-okay.

The capsule containing Ham landed on the waves of the Atlantic Ocean. Helicopter pilots, remembering that the monkey Ol' Reliable had been lost at sea, raced to it. Even so, it took over three hours to reach the capsule, which floated and bobbed on the sea as it had been designed to do. Frogmen were lowered into the sea. They quickly put inflatable rings around the capsule to keep it from sinking when opened. Finally they opened up the space capsule. There was Ham, bright, alert, and pleased to see them after his historic journey.

NASA officials, scientists, and especially doctors breathed sighs of relief. They were now convinced that a man could go into space and not only survive, but do useful work. Medical space recordings showed that Ham had suffered no ill effects.

With the success of Ham's mission under their belts, NASA scientists worked at breakneck pace for the United States to put the first man in space. The launching was scheduled for May 1961—a mere four months after Ham's trip. The astronaut was selected and prepared. Then, once again, the Soviet Union beat NASA to the punch.

YURI GAGARIN ORBITS THE EARTH

On April 12, 1961, dawn appeared over the Russian steppes. As the sun slowly rose and began shining on the rooftops of Tyuratam, Russia, some men and women fished in the nearby Syr Darya River, while others went to work in melon and grain fields. Who could have guessed that a turning point in history would soon take place a mere five kilometers away?

Yuri Gagarin

The man who first orbited our planet came from a small rural area that had hardly changed since the Middle Ages, where the houses were still made of logs and thatched roofs. Yuri Alekseyevich Gagarin was born March 9, 1934, on a collective farm about 100 miles from Moscow. Until age seven, he spent a peaceful, healthy life in the country, where he played among trees and fields of flax and wheat.

In 1941 the Nazi army overran the area, and the Gagarin family apparently became refugees fleeing from the Germans. After the war, Gagarin returned and went to school. Later he went to a vocational school in a suburb of Moscow, near a large airplane factory.

The sight of the airplanes being tested thrilled Gagarin, and he dreamed of a career in aviation.

While attending the industrial college of Saratov, he spent his spare time learning to fly with an aero club. He graduated from college with high honors in 1957 and joined the Air Force, where he eventually entered the cosmonaut program.

On the morning of April 12, 1961, the nose of a gigantic rocket pointed toward the sky. Its nose cone usually carried a warhead, but on that strange and peaceful morning, it carried instead Major Yuri Gagarin of the Soviet Air Force. To emphasize the peaceful mission he was about to embark upon, the nose cone had been renamed *Vostok*—"Swallow," in English—for the swift-flying bird.

At 9:07 A.M. (Moscow time), flames shot out from the engines of the rocket, and it lifted off. A few minutes later, Gagarin was in orbit, drifting weightlessly over the earth, high above the atmosphere. He was the first man ever to look down on the earth's atmosphere and see its blue edge on the horizon, to look down on the incredible blue oceans, to see the sunset and sunrise coloring the vast horizons, and to look into the incredible black void of endless space.

The trip took him 188 miles above the earth at his highest point and 109 miles at his lowest point. The spacecraft traveled at 17,000 miles per hour.

Gagarin not only sat watching the passing scenes from the window of the *Vostok*, he also drank water, ate food, and worked on the control buttons of various instruments.

The spacecraft was a mere seven and a half feet in diameter and weighed about 5,290 pounds. Inside was normal air at atmospheric pressure. Gagarin circled the earth once. The historic flight lasted a mere 108 minutes.

The Russians were secretive about Gagarin's trip, but in a radio communication he made while over South America he was heard to say that his flight was proceeding normally.

After the flight, Gagarin said that he was quite surprised to see the earth's horizon was not straight but curved. He enjoyed and was awed by the transition of sky colors on Earth to the velvety blackness of space. All in all, he said, his emotion was one of joy.

Immediately after landing, Gagarin went to see the Soviet premier Nikita Khrushchev, who, it is said, smothered him with hugs and kisses. In Moscow, Gagarin received a hero's welcome. He was made a hero of the Soviet

Union and showered with honors. There were parades and gun salutes.

In spite of the cold war, people all over the world, Americans included, were amazed and excited by Gagarin's feat. His flight made important progress for humankind.

On March 27, 1968, Major Yuri Gagarin was killed in an automobile accident, and the world mourned his loss.

5

The Race
to the Moon

After Gagarin's success, Nikita Khrushchev quickly left the
Soviet Union and went on visits to various countries, pro-
claiming Soviet science and power. Many countries, especially those in the Third World, looked up to Russia as
they had never done before.

PRESIDENT JOHN F. KENNEDY AND THE
MOON RACE

The new young American president, John F. Kennedy,
was disturbed by the Russian achievement, and by the
world's reaction to it. Since taking office in January 1961,
Kennedy had pondered what to do about America's space
program and how to react to the Russian successes.

Kennedy was not pleased with the lukewarm program
he had inherited from Eisenhower. He, along with many
senators and especially his new vice-president, Lyndon
Johnson, saw the Russian achievements as a foreign policy
threat. Kennedy knew that the rest of the world saw the

success of the USSR as proof-positive that Russia was the stronger of the two superpowers, the one that looked more toward the future. The Soviet Union appeared to have industrial and scientific might, and a disciplined and efficient economy. As long as most nations believed that the USSR was the major superpower, Kennedy feared, they would back away from the United States and not give it full support.

In his first hectic weeks in office, Kennedy spent whatever hours he could reading about space, rockets, the astronauts, satellites, and related subjects. When he had the time, he held lengthy discussions with space experts.

World events were rushing forward. The triumphs of the USSR were daily strengthening the Soviets. They were making political and economic gains. In addition to the Soviet achievements in space, there were threats in Southeast Asia. In Kennedy's view, world problems were interrelated, and the Soviet space achievements allowed the Communists in Southeast Asia to be bolder.

Kennedy felt challenged to prove to the world, in a spectacular way, that the United States was the most powerful of the superpowers and the one with the biggest industrial and scientific might. He met with experts and advisers to discuss ways to do this. He considered urban renewal, but decided against it because other nations would not see or feel the results. He considered new methods for desalinating seawater, so that fresh water could be obtained from the oceans. This would have been a great feat, but he felt it lacked human drama and excitement. Then he considered the space program. At first he believed, as did his advisers, that *anything* the United States did in space would look as though it were merely second best. The Soviet Union seemed to have too much of a lead. To come in second was not good enough.

Then Kennedy turned to Lyndon Johnson to find a solution to the problem of America's response to the threat.

Johnson, forever a space fan, threw himself wholeheartedly into his new assignment. He talked to virtually hundreds of men and women in industry, NASA, politics, top universities, economics, the diplomatic corps, and elsewhere. His vitality was unending, and he left no stone unturned.

Lyndon Johnson talked unofficially with Wernher von Braun about the Russian rockets. Von Braun pointed out that if the Soviet Union was to send men to the moon, they would have to spend years designing, manufacturing, and testing a completely new type of rocket. Von Braun was certain that the Soviets could not prepare for going to the moon any more easily than the Americans could.

Though the Soviet space program had much more experience with large rockets than did NASA, they had never made a rocket large enough to go to the moon. They knew less than NASA did about the computers, radio communications, and machinery necessary for such a mission. And it appeared they might also have difficulties setting up launchpads and building the rest of the backup equipment needed for a flight to the moon. Von Braun's own unofficial opinion was that the United States had about an even chance of beating the Soviet Union to the moon.

On April 14, 1961—two days after Yuri Gagarin's flight—Kennedy held an important cabinet meeting to discuss the possibility of a moon race. He asked the key question: Can the United States get to the moon first? Can we build and put in place the proposed *Saturn* rocket before the Russians can build a moon rocket? A major concern, he said, was the sheer cost of it. His advisers had told him that to get men to the moon and back would cost $40 billion.

As the meeting came to a close, Kennedy said in a low voice, "There is nothing more important."

But soon he was faced with a more pressing concern. An American-backed invasion of Cuba, at the Bay of Pigs, failed disastrously, further damaging the United States in the eyes of the world.

Although one dramatic event after another helped to bring the president close to a decision, it was not until an American went into space on May 5, 1961, giving Kennedy confidence in the American space program, that he finally made up his mind.

THE FIRST AMERICAN IN SPACE

Despite a calm and professional appearance, NASA officials were extraordinarily nervous about the first manned flight.

Appearing coolest of all was Commander Alan B. Shepard, Jr., of the U.S. Navy—the astronaut chosen by NASA to be America's first man in space.

Alan B. Shepard

Alan Bartlett Shepard was born November 18, 1923, in East Derry, New Hampshire. He received his elementary school education in a one-room school in East Derry, where he was liked by students and teachers. As a cadet at the United States Naval Academy, he was a member of the Navy varsity crew team for three years. In 1944 Shepard graduated and went immediately into World War II, where he served on the destroyer USS *Cogswell*.

In 1947 he received his wings. He entered the Navy Test Pilot School at Patuxent River, Maryland, in 1950, and by 1958 Shepard had flown 3,700 hours.

It was a tense, thrilling, but fearful moment when the American astronaut Alan B. Shepard got into the *Mercury* capsule, named *Freedom 7*, on May 5, 1961. (The original astronauts named their space capsules and always added a "7" to the name, for the seven astronauts.) The eyes of the world were on him.

Thousands of people stood in the hot Florida sun to wait for the blast-off. At 9:34 A.M., after a long, four hour and fourteen minute wait, the countdown was given as tens of millions of Americans watched on television or listened

Astronaut Alan Shepard, the first American to go into space. Later, as the commander of *Apollo 14*, he went to the moon. Here he stands next to the *Apollo 14* emblem.

to the radio. Flames shot out from the engines, and the *Redstone 3* rocket shivered and then slowly moved upward. Gracefully it gathered speed until it reached a maximum height of 116.5 miles.

The flight lasted a mere 15 minutes and 22 seconds and covered a distance of 303.8 miles. Shepard was weightless for only five minutes. While high above the earth, he radioed his experience to Mission Control: "What a beautiful view!"

As the spacecraft plunged through the atmosphere and slowed down, its speed dropped from 5,000 to 500 miles per hour in only 30 seconds. Shepard felt a pull against him equal to ten times the force of gravity. Most people could not endure such a G force, but because of his physical strength and training, he easily survived it without harm.

The capsule landed on the ocean and was picked up by frogmen. Shepard had survived in perfect health and had been able to go through a short work schedule even while weightless. He said after the flight, "The only complaint I have was the flight was not long enough."

Shepard became a national hero and was given ticker-tape parades in New York City and in Los Angeles. Almost every American knew his name, and so did people around the world. Nikita Khrushchev sent congratulations from the Soviet Union. A crowd of 250,000 stood along Pennsylvania Avenue in Washington, D.C., on May 8 to greet the astronaut hero. He met with President Kennedy and was given the civilian Distinguished Service Medal of the National Aeronautics and Space Administration.

URGENT NATIONAL NEED

The success of the Mercury Redstone 3 mission was just the stimulus President Kennedy needed to come to a decision about a race to the moon.

On May 25, just three weeks after Alan Shepard's flight, Kennedy gave a speech on "Urgent National Needs." He billed it as a "second State of the Union" message. It went down in history as a speech that changed the course of human events.

Interestingly, Kennedy did not begin with even a mention of space. He saved his thoughts on space for the ending. Then he said:

> The dramatic achievements in space which occurred in recent weeks should have made clear to us all the impact of this adventure on the minds of men everywhere. . . .
>
> Now is the time to take longer strides, time for a great new American enterprise, time for this nation to take a clearly leading role in space achievement, which in many ways may hold the key to our future on Earth. . . .
>
> Recognizing the head start obtained by the Soviets with their large rocket engines, which gives them many months lead time, and recognizing the likelihood that they will exploit this lead time

for some time to come in still more impressive successes, we nevertheless are required to make new efforts of our own. For while we cannot guarantee that we shall one day be first, we can guarantee that any failure to make this effort will find us last. We take an additional risk by making it in full view of the world. . . .

I therefore ask the Congress, above and beyond the increases I have earlier requested for space activities, to provide the funds which are needed to meet the following national goals:

First, I believe that this nation should commit itself to achieving the goal, before this decade is out, of landing a man on the moon and returning him safely to Earth. . . .

Congress backed Kennedy and provided the necessary funds. And so it was that world events were to help determine that Americans would someday go to the moon.

PLANNING THE TRIP TO THE MOON

It was one thing to say that we'd go to the moon, and another to figure out how.

Could human beings survive for days in space? Yuri Gagarin's flight proved that a man could stay in space for a couple of hours, but men going to the moon would have to stay alive in space for days at a time. What might happen? Would radioactivity in space kill them? Would weightlessness weaken them? Could they think well enough after a few hours in space? Would they become ill? Could space suits be manufactured that would allow them to walk on the moon?

Then there was the matter of what the rocks and soil on the moon were like. No one knew. Some thought that the moon's surface was mostly covered with lava that had long ago hardened into solid rock. Others believed that the moon was covered with a thick layer of dust, which in places could be hundreds of feet or even miles deep. They feared that a spacecraft landing on the moon would sink into the dust, much the way a rock would sink into the ocean. If the moon were covered with such a dust, it was obvious that no one could land.

Then there was the most basic problem of all: how to get to the moon. Several suggestions were made, and NASA considered each carefully.

One way called for a huge rocket carrying the astronauts in a module to land on the moon and then take off again from the moon's surface. This plan was discarded because the huge size of the rocket would make it too difficult to test and maneuver, among other problems.

Another way was to send two rockets into Earth orbit, one carrying astronauts and the other carrying mostly fuel. The two rockets would meet in orbit, and the astronauts would fuel their rocket. With the additional fuel, the astronauts could make it to the moon and back.

While NASA considered this plan, a 41-year-old engineer named John C. Houbolt imagined another way.

The idea he worked out with his associates called for the use of the tried-and-true *Saturn 5* rocket. It would lift two capsules, one a command module for carrying three astronauts and the other a detachable lunar module that would be a landing craft. When in space the command vehicle and lunar module would fly joined together toward the moon. By slowing down the command module with rockets, the astronauts would orbit the moon. Once in orbit, two of the three astronauts would crawl out of the command module and get into the lunar module. They would separate it from the command ship and make a landing on the moon.

On the moon the two astronauts would get out of the lunar lander, explore the area next to the lander, and then get back into the lunar lander. The top half of the lunar lander would hold an ascent stage containing a rocket and space for the two astronauts. The ascent stage would detach from the lower half. Once it had detached, the two astronauts could start rocket engines and take off from the moon, leaving the lower half of the lunar module behind. Using their tiny rocket ship, they would leave the surface of the moon, meet the command module, and hook up with it once more. The two astronauts would crawl back into the command module to join their companion who had stayed behind. The lunar ascent stage would be set free to crash on the moon. Then the three astronauts would fly back to Earth.

Houbolt's plan sounded very complicated, and in fact NASA officials dismissed it with harsh words at first. Too many things had to be done. Too many orbits. Too many transfers. Much too risky. All sorts of things could go wrong.

As other plans were proposed and dropped, some scientists saw that Houbolt's plan had its good points. Most of the equipment would be lightweight and small. Each piece could be easily and thoroughly tested on Earth before it went into space. Much less fuel would be needed to get to the moon and back. It would cost less than other methods. And, finally, with no better alternatives in sight, NASA decided to use Houbolt's plan, called LOR, for lunar-orbit rendezvous. *Rendezvous* is French for "meeting."

Once NASA decided on LOR, the agency knew just what to do. They would begin with a mission for one man to orbit the earth in the *Mercury* space capsule, which had already been designed. Next, because the *Mercury* module held only one astronaut, they'd design and build a larger one, called *Gemini*, to hold two astronauts. They would test it in space, and the *Gemini* astronauts would practice leaving the capsule and walking in space. Finally they would build the *Apollo* space capsules, which could hold three astronauts, and test them in Earth orbit and in moon orbit.

Once the *Apollo* astronauts and equipment passed those tests, they'd send astronauts to the moon for a landing.

GRISSOM'S NEAR MISS

While sweeping plans were being made for a trip to the moon, NASA proceeded with Project Mercury as scheduled. A follow-up flight to Alan Shepard's success had been scheduled for July 21, 1961. That day, Virgil I. Grissom, known to all as "Gus," went into space in a *Mercury* capsule, which he named *Liberty Bell 7*. He reached an altitude of 118 miles and landed 303 miles from the lift-off point.

The mission went smoothly. In space, Grissom reported that he saw a star, which he believed was Capella. Looking out his window at one point in the 15-minute flight, he said he was amazed that Cape Canaveral looked so close though it was one hundred miles below him. The *Liberty Bell 7* hit the water, Grissom later reported, with

Splashdown. All of the *Mercury, Gemini,* and *Apollo* spacecraft landed back on Earth in splashdowns much like this one (*Apollo 15's* landing in the Pacific Ocean).

"a pretty good bump." As helicopters came over to the capsule to lift it up, Grissom "took the detonator cap and pulled the safety pin." This meant that he had prepared the explosive bolts on the hatch to explode as planned and loosen the hatch so that he could get out. He was supposed to wait until the helicopter had lowered a line and had the capsule in grip before he finally set off the explosives.

Then an unexpected thing occurred. The explosives went off and the hatch opened before the helicopter arrived. Grissom was stunned to see blue sky above him. He remained seated in the capsule for a few moments, but seawater began to come in. Fearing it would soon sink, Grissom got out.

A helicopter tried to lift the capsule, but too much water had entered and weighed it down. Unable to lift it, the helicopter loosened the lines and the capsule sank.

Grissom swam about for a few minutes, but his space suit began to fill with water, and he soon found himself fighting for life. Several times a helicopter tried to get a line to him, but Grissom was blown away by the backlash from the propellers. Just in time, the pilot turned the helicopter and let the line out in a new direction. Grissom grabbed it and was rescued.

After in-depth research, a final Project Mercury report stated: "The cause of the malfunction has never been determined."

In spite of the accident and near loss of an astronaut, the flight had gone well, and NASA was ready to advance to the next dramatic step: the orbit of the earth.

AN AMERICAN ORBITS THE EARTH

Lieutenant Colonel John H. Glenn was chosen to orbit the earth, a choice that would assure him of fame. Scott Carpenter was his backup man. If for any reason Glenn could not go, Carpenter would. All seven of the astronauts, in fact, were equally qualified to orbit the earth. Any one of them could have been chosen. In the end, fate as much as anything else played a part in Glenn's selection.

John Glenn of *Friendship 7*

Glenn was born on July 18, 1921, in Cambridge, Ohio. From the beginning he was a "wonder boy." An honor student in high school, he was also the class president and took a lead role in the senior class play. He was deeply religious and joined many church groups.

After graduating from high school, Glenn went to Muskingum College in New Concord, where he was a member of the football team.

He learned to fly in a naval program for civilians at New Philadelphia, Ohio. Later he went on to complete flight school at the Naval Air Training Center in Corpus Christi, Texas. He joined the Marines and became a marine fighter pilot.

During World War II, Glenn flew 59 missions in F4U fighters in the Marshall Islands campaign, earning two Distinguished Flying Crosses and ten Air Medals. In the Korean War, he flew 90 missions between February and September 1953 and won his third and fourth Distinguished Flying Crosses and eight more Air Medals.

In July 1957, he set a speed record with a flight from Los Angeles to Bennett Field in New York, making the trip in three hours, 23 minutes, and 8.4 seconds. For this achievement, Glenn was given yet another Distinguished Flying Cross.

Glenn was promoted to the rank of Lieutenant Colonel on April 1, 1959. Eight days later he was one of the first of the seven astronauts chosen by NASA, and two and a half years later, he was selected to be the first American astronaut to orbit the earth.

The launch was scheduled for February 20, 1962. A huge crowd gathered that day at Cape Canaveral, Florida, including many foreign ambassadors, American high officials, and visiting Russian dignitaries. Glenn settled himself down into the contoured couch inside the *Mercury* space capsule, which he named *Friendship 7*. He wore a simple space suit, of the type used by high-altitude test pilots. (Only if the pressure in the capsule failed would he inflate it.) Above him was a small window.

After ignition, huge flames roared from the rocket engines. At 9:47 A.M., the *Atlas-D* rocket slowly moved upward and then gathered speed. Glenn was carried higher into the sky than any other American had been, reaching an altitude of 163 miles above Earth. The *Mercury* capsule released from the rocket moved silently, smoothly, weightlessly through space, high above the earth's atmosphere.

As directed, Glenn turned his capsule around so that the heat shields would face forward. This was a necessary safety measure. In case Glenn blacked out or could not control the spacecraft, it would slowly lose altitude and reenter the earth's atmosphere by itself, delivering him, it was hoped, safely back to Earth.

During every moment of his flight, Glenn was busy working controls, keeping notes, eating, drinking water, and talking via radio to Navy and NASA ships at sea and to tracking stations in such places as Florida, Africa, Australia, and Hawaii. His first report was radioed back to fellow astronaut Alan Shepard at Cape Canaveral: "Zero G and I feel fine."

The spacecraft flew over Bermuda, where Glenn picked up another NASA radio operator, and then over the Canary Islands, where he took his own blood pressure and described how being weightless felt. His blood pressure and heart rate were normal. He moved his head in "head exercises" to see if he got dizzy, reached out and touched things to see if weightlessness made a difference in his hand-eye coordination, and ate to see whether he could swallow food while weightless. He passed all the tests easily.

Astronaut John H. Glenn, Jr., dressed in his space suit. Glenn was the first American to orbit the earth.

As he flew over the Sahara, he saw enormous dust storms below him swirling across the desert. Later he saw the smoke of brush fires and talked to a radio operator in Kano, Nigeria. On he flew in orbit as only two men had ever done before. He picked up a radio in Zanzibar and again did a check on his blood pressure, sending the information back to Zanzibar.

Thirty-six minutes into the flight, Glenn entered into his first sunset, quickly followed by night. He explained to listeners below that he could see the night horizon. Then

53

he was all alone, out of radio contact with anyone. Glenn marveled at the cloud formations far away, through which he could see stars shining. He spoke of the view into a tape recorder. He described how the stars jumped toward him out of the blackness of space. He was awed at the way he could see the different colors of ocean currents far below him. Like Gagarin, Glenn enjoyed the colors of the earth's atmosphere and the strange sunrise and sunset.

Glenn picked up radio communication again with Muchea, Australia. He heard a familiar voice on the radio. It was fellow astronaut Leroy Gordon Cooper, known to all as Gordo. Asked how he was doing, Glenn answered, "We're doing really fine up here."

Glenn reported seeing the constellation the Pleiades. (The observation of stars is important so that celestial navigation can be carried out if needed.)

While over the Pacific Ocean, he communicated with radio operators on Canton Island and described "the brilliant, brilliant red" of a sunset. Then he mentioned something most peculiar. He saw tiny white specks about one-sixteenth of an inch across all around him. They stretched away in all directions for miles. He said they had the color of a bright firefly. The specks were about "seven or eight feet apart." To this day, no one is certain what he saw, but scientists assume they were flecks chipping off the capsule.

Coming around the globe toward his starting point, Glenn passed over Hawaii and Guymas, Mexico, and then he was back above Cape Canaveral. He had orbited the world. Ground observers noted the perfect flight. They were pleased. Everything was successful and going along perfectly. NASA gave him a "go" for two more orbits.

Out over the Atlantic Ocean, Glenn saw the wake of a ship—an important observation. Not only were scientists and NASA officials curious to know what one could see from such a height, but so were military officials, who had wondered what strategic information could be gained in space.

Once more he did "head exercises" to see if he felt dizzy or nauseated. Glenn continued to feel fine.

At two hours and 19 minutes into the flight, he received a puzzling radio message from "the Indian Ocean ship." He was ordered to keep his landing-bag switch in the off position. Glenn told the radio operators that the switch had been and was in the off position.

Unknown to Glenn, tensions were mounting at Cape Canaveral. There were indications that the MA-6 landing bag (which would cushion the capsule's splashdown in the ocean) might have opened too early. That could only have happened if the locks that held the heat shield had opened up. Had the heat shield fallen off, the capsule moving through the atmosphere would have burned up, killing Glenn. At the time, Glenn had no way of knowing whether those locks had opened or not, because there were no indicators for the locks in the capsule.

The project directors—Walter Williams, Christopher Kraft, and Robert Gilruth—felt terrible anxiety. They had no idea whether the signals they were getting were accurate.

Glenn was unaware of the concern back at Mission Control. Over Woomera, Australia, he reported that his eyesight was still acute. (Doctors had long wondered how human eyes would adjust to weightlessness.)

Then more problems arose. The gyroscopes were giving Glenn wrong readings. The timekeeper was off by a second, which sounds minor, but he was covering almost seven miles in a second. Glenn didn't worry. He got an accurate time check from a ground-based radio station and corrected the gyroscope.

Not until Glenn made his last pass over Hawaii was he told for the first time that indicators showed problems with his landing bag. Again he was ordered to keep the switch in the off position. Controllers believed that if the landing bag was retained, then the straps holding it might also hold the heat shield on—if it was still on.

At four hours, 32 minutes, and 37 seconds into his flight, Glenn fired the retro-rockets. The dangerous descent had begun.

Because the automatic controls were proving unreliable, Glenn was ordered to take manual control of the space capsule. He would pilot it down. He managed to enter the atmosphere at a low angle to keep G forces low.

Because of complex atmospheric conditions in the ionosphere, Glenn was out of radio contact with anyone on Earth for four and a half minutes. Well knowing that he might be on a death trip, he hummed a little tune to himself and steadied the capsule as it plunged downward. Through his window he saw nothing but flames leaping by. They blazed on the heat shield, eating it away. A fireball grew around the capsule as air friction heated it. Glenn could not determine whether the flames were eating away at the heat shield or the entire capsule. At any moment he expected them to work their way through the capsule and surround him.

But the heat shield held through reentry while the earth's atmosphere slowed the capsule on schedule. Glenn survived.

At four hours, 47 minutes, and 16 seconds into the flight, Glenn's radio came alive. It was astronaut Alan Shepard. "How do you read?" asked Shepard.

Glenn answered, "Loud and clear. How me? Mercury Control, come back to life."

Shepard asked, "How are you doing?"

Glenn answered, "Oh, pretty good."

At 45,000 feet Glenn released a parachute and at 10,000 feet another one. The capsule gently floated down from the sky.

When the capsule hit the water, Glenn radioed out, "Friendship 7. Impact."

Twenty minutes later, *Friendship 7*, with Glenn inside it, was on the deck of the Navy ship USS *Noa*.

When Glenn emerged from the capsule, he commented, "It sure was hot in there."

America cheered Glenn's safe return and proclaimed him a true hero. He was showered with confetti in ticker-tape parades. President Kennedy invited him to the White House and praised his accomplishments in a speech from the Rose Garden. Glenn addressed a joint session of Congress and received countless medals.

Now the long years of effort had paid off. The Mercury Project proved the capsule designs to be sound. (Actually, the Soviet Union would later copy the designs.) A pilot could live and function in space. He could also control a space capsule, at least to some degree, while in orbit and while reentering the atmosphere. Men could withstand punishing G forces and still function normally in space. Radio communications worked to and from the orbiting capsule. Recovery of the capsules (aside from one loss) was feasible and presented only minor problems.

But not all the success could be explained in terms of hardware and physical accomplishments. There was, of course, a psychological boost. These flights gave NASA personnel faith in their own ideas about science and engineering. Their plans had been sound. With new confidence, NASA decided to move ahead to the Gemini Project after confirming their success with three more orbital missions: on May 24, 1962, Scott Carpenter made three orbits of the earth; on October 3, 1962, Walter Schirra made six orbits; and on May 15, 1963, Gordon Cooper made the longest flight in a *Mercury* capsule, orbiting the earth 22 times.

So ended the amazing Mercury Project. All was "go" for Gemini.

6

Gemini and Apollo: Space Is Mastered

SPACE ADVANCEMENTS WORLDWIDE

How quickly the world had changed. NASA had succeeded not only in manned flights into space, but also in unmanned space probes. The remarkable American *Ranger 7*, launched July 28, 1964, actually went to the moon and sent back 4,300 photographs before its preplanned crash on the moon's surface. *Syncom 2*, an American communications satellite, succeeded in receiving messages from the earth and sending them back. Worldwide communications were revolutionized. The American *OSO I*, a solar observing satellite, studied the sun. On August 26, 1962, a joint American-British satellite, *Ariel 1*, was successfully launched to study the earth's highest layers of the atmosphere. With it, England had become part of the Space Age. On September 29, 1962, Canada and the United States sent up *Alouette* to study the earth's ionosphere in a joint mission.

Still, the Soviet Union remained ahead, with an awesome lead. As early as January and September 1959, the Soviets had sent *Luna 1* and *Luna 2* to the moon. *Luna 3*, launched on October 4, 1959, circled the moon and took photographs of its far side—the side we never see from Earth. (This feat seemed so unbelievable at the time that many American scientists declared it a fake.) On November 1, 1963, the Soviets launched *Polyot 1*, which was able to maneuver in space, changing positions on commands from the ground.

It was with their spectacular manned flights that the Soviets showed their finest capabilities. *Vostok 3*, launched August 11, 1962, with Andrian Nikolayev on board, orbited the earth 64 times. On June 14, 1963, *Vostok 5* went aloft carrying V. F. Bykovskiy. This spacecraft circled the earth 81 times, and was aloft for 119 hours and six minutes. On March 18, 1965, the Soviets sent aloft *Voskhod 2* with A.A. Leonov and Pavel I. Belyayev aboard. During the time it orbited the earth, Leonov took the first space walk.

The pressure kept up. But NASA held its ground. NASA and Lyndon Johnson, the new American president following Kennedy's assassination, kept to the original plans for the moon race. They felt that a steady, sure pace would lead the United States to its goal of reaching the moon before the Soviet Union.

NASA expanded its facilities, hired more people, and brought in two new groups of astronauts: nine more in September 1962 and 14 in October 1963. The original seven were no longer an exclusive club.

TWO MEN IN A SPACECRAFT: THE GEMINI PROGRAM

The goal of the Gemini project, begun in late 1961, was to see how men could live in space for much longer periods of time—long enough to go to the moon and back. Another important goal of the project was to figure out how two spacecraft could rendezvous in space.

59

The *Gemini* capsule would differ from the *Mercury* capsule in many important ways. First of all, of course, it had to be large enough to carry two astronauts, not one, as well as their water, food, oxygen, and so on. And it had to be maneuverable—the astronauts would have to steer it and make it go faster, slower, higher, or lower, so that the rendezvous could be made correctly.

The *Gemini* capsule was far larger and more complex than any space capsule, Russian or American, ever built. It weighed 8,000 pounds—exactly four tons. Cone-shaped like the *Mercury* capsule, it was 11 feet at its longest and 7 feet 6 inches at its widest.

But the ingenious capsule was only one part of the Gemini project. Of equal importance were the space suits.

The space suit had to stand up to extraordinarily difficult conditions never before encountered by any human being. Once an astronaut was out of a spacecraft, on the moon or while in orbit, he would meet with severe conditions. Empty space is a vacuum. He would be unable to take a breath of air, for none was there. Without a suit he'd be unconscious in a matter of seconds and quickly die. His blood might boil. (Water boils at a lower and lower temperature at great heights. At about 60,000 feet above the earth and beyond, human blood can boil.) So, the suit had to contain air for the astronauts to breathe, and air pressure to keep the astronauts' blood from boiling. With air pressure in the suit, a weakly made suit could balloon outward so much that the astronaut could not move. In order to avoid that, the suit needed to be reinforced at many points.

The astronauts also had to contend with extreme cold and extreme heat. The sun on one side of the astronaut could heat him to over 245°F. But the cold darkness of space on his other side would freeze him to -279°F. The suit had to be well insulated against both heat and cold. To keep the astronaut cool enough in his thick insulation, the space suit was equipped with special underwear containing numerous small tubes that carried cool water.

In space, tiny meteoroids, about the size of a grain of sand, travel far faster than any bullet on Earth, reaching speeds of about 20 to 35 miles per second. One of them could go through most fabrics. The space suit was covered with a tough outer skin and some inner skins as well to protect against a meteoroid puncture.

The glare of the sun is much worse in space than on Earth. The suit had to have a see-through window in front and a sunglass screen as well.

Sound is carried through the air by sound waves. But because there is no air in space to carry sound, neither is there any sound. The space suit, then, was equipped with a radio, so that one astronaut could talk to another.

The suit had to allow astronauts to drink water, eat a snack, and eliminate body wastes. Because doctors wanted to monitor the astronauts while they walked on the moon or went out into space, there had to be ways of attaching medical devices to the suit.

The space suit became one of the extraordinary achievements of the whole space program. An inner suit made of spandex was embedded with the tiny water-carrying tubes. Over that was another layer of spandex that fitted loosely, like a shirt. Attached to it was wiring for medical instruments. It also carried oxygen ducts. Next was a layer of heat-resistant nylon, and a pressure-holding layer of neoprene to keep the suit from ballooning. On the outside of the suit was a thermal/meteoroid garment. It reflected heat and protected the astronaut from the swift-flying meteoroids. If they hit the suit their energy was absorbed by a special type of Dacron.

The helmet was large enough to let the astronaut move his head in all directions. There was a pillow in it so that an astronaut lying down could rest his head. To protect him from the glare of the sun and ultraviolet light, which is intense in space, the visor was covered with a thin layer of gold.

A tube near the astronaut's mouth was connected to

a water bag, so that he could drink. A tube of candy was also near his mouth. He could squeeze it to get a snack. A radio near his mouth enabled him to communicate with a fellow astronaut near him and with Mission Control on Earth.

The oxygen supply was carried in a big pack on the astronaut's back.

The whole space suit weighed 200 pounds on Earth, but less than 35 pounds on the moon, where the pull of gravity is so much less.

One can hardly praise the final, successful space suit enough. It virtually opened up the moon to exploration—not to mention Mars and other planetary satellites in the future. The suit was as important as a rocket or a lunar lander.

On April 8, 1964, the *Gemini 1* capsule went into orbit around the earth with no one in it. NASA needed to know just how the larger and more complex capsule would act in space, how well it could change height and direction, and how well communications networks would function. Above all, NASA scientists wanted to know if it could come through the earth's atmosphere without damage and land safely.

The first unmanned flight was a success. Another unmanned flight took *Gemini 2* into space on January 19, 1965. This suborbital flight tested the heat shield. Again the results were excellent.

On March 23, 1965, Virgil I. Grissom and John W. Young orbited the earth three times in the *Gemini 3*. For the first time ever, astronauts changed orbits and moved a space capsule higher and lower into new orbits as they circled the earth.

WALKING IN SPACE

To orbit the earth in a spacecraft seemed the height of adventure and daring. But on June 3, 1965, a far more daring and, in a way, strange adventure took place. A human being, protected only by a space suit, would climb out of the hatch of an orbiter traveling at almost seven miles per second and float, alone, out into space. There, attached to the spacecraft only by a tube carrying oxygen and communications, the astronaut would "fly" on his own. Nothing would be below him for a hundred miles. Around him would be infinite space, dotted only by the moon, planets, and distant galaxies.

The man NASA selected for America's first walk in space was Edward H. White. He would be accompanied by James A. McDivitt in *Gemini 4*.

Edward H. White: Spacewalker

Edward White was born in San Antonio, Texas, on November 14, 1930. As the son of a retired major general of the United States Air Force, he moved from one town to another with his family.

When he was a small child, his father took him for a ride in an AT-6 trainer airplane. Young Edward was thrilled by the flight and would never forget it. From then on he was interested in aviation.

After high school, White went to West Point, where he ran the 400-meter hurdles in record-breaking time. He almost made the U.S. Olympic team. After graduating in 1952, White followed his love of aviation and joined the Air Force. He attended flight school in Florida.

White wanted to become an astronaut but needed to further his education. He went as a member of the Air Force to the University of Michigan where he received a masters degree in aeronautical engineering in 1959. Later he flew KC-135 cargo planes that were used to demonstrate the effects of weightlessness to astronauts. White's job was to fly the plane high and then drop it rapidly.

On September 17, 1962, NASA accepted nine new astronauts, including White. His experiences with weightlessness (he figured he had spent a total of five hours in a

Edward H. White II, the first American astronaut to "walk" in space.

weightless condition) paid off. In 1964 NASA decided that White and Major James A. McDivitt, an old friend of White's, would go into space, and that White would try out the space walk.

That day in June, White found himself out in space, floating in the emptiness of eternity with only a long cord attaching him to the spacecraft. The earth lay 135 miles below him. Sometimes he looked down at it as he flew over; at other times he was upside down looking at the pitch-black sky and brilliant stars.

White was supposed to "walk" in space for 12 minutes, but he was so overjoyed by the feeling of floating out there that he could not bring himself to return to the spacecraft for 20 minutes.

His conversations with McDivitt, who was inside *Gemini 4*, were broadcast live all over the United States. Some 194,000,000 people heard his remarks with wonder and amusement.

"I'm very thankful in having the experience to be first," he said. Then with a trace of humor he said to McDivitt, "Right now, I'm actually walking across the top of the spacecraft. I'm on top of the window."

McDivitt, in mock anger, answered, "You just smeared my windshield, you dirty dog." White somersaulted away to float free.

After White had floated along, crossing hundreds of miles of the United States in a matter of minutes, a message came in from Houston. "The flight director wants for White to get back in."

White made no move. Down in Houston, Grissom called, "Gemini 4, Gemini. Get back in."

"Well," McDivitt urged, "get back in."

Then, to the amazement of McDivitt and Houston officials, White said, "I don't want to come back to you."

McDivitt was frustrated, and Grissom was worried.

Reluctantly, White finally reentered the *Gemini 4* spacecraft, saying, "It's the saddest moment of my life."

White had floated across the entire length of the United States plus another 3,000 miles.

On June 7, 1965, four days after it was launched, *Gemini 4* safely landed. President Johnson talked to White and McDivitt on the telephone and later nominated them for promotion to lieutenant colonel. The two were given the Distinguished Service Medal of NASA and astronaut's wings.

The public watched on television as White floated a hundred miles above the earth. It was like a fantasy, and few activities of the space program captured the imagination of the public as did White's walk in space.

NASA officials were also thrilled, but for different reasons. White's space walk had opened a door to the future. A person could survive on the moon. Astronauts could go outside a space capsule and make repairs on it. In the future, it was clear, astronauts would be able to do much more than airplane pilots could. A pilot of a 747 cannot, after all, walk out on the wing and make repairs while the plane is in flight. But an astronaut could work outside a spacecraft moving over seven miles per second. A new era in the space program had arrived.

MORE GEMINI SUCCESSES

For the public, the space walks were the most dramatic of the Gemini missions, but there were many other successes as well. Starting December 4, 1965, Frank Borman and James A. Lovell made a world-record flight in *Gemini 7*. For 14 days they stayed in space, making 206 orbits of the earth. They met with *Gemini 6*, launched December 15, 1965, which carried Walter M. Schirra and Thomas P. Stafford. This was the first American space rendezvous.

The Gemini 8 mission also called for two vehicles to dock—to meet in air and attach. Neil Armstrong was the pilot of the *Gemini 8* capsule. Right after docking with the target vehicle, the spacecraft rolled dangerously. For a while it seemed that Armstrong was headed for disaster, but he was finally able to gain control over the spinning space vehicle. To that date, it was the closest call in NASA's history.

There were many other triumphs in the Gemini program. With each success taking NASA a step closer to the moon, NASA officials were ready to go ahead with the Apollo program.

THE APOLLO PROGRAM

Ever since NASA had accepted Houbolt's moon landing plans, they had figured on three men going to the moon.

The three astronauts would be in the command module, a cone-shaped vehicle 12 feet 10 inches wide at its widest part and 10 feet 7 inches tall. Each astronaut had a couch. On the armrests were controls that operated and guided the capsule. Inside the capsule they would wear lightweight clothing. Their space suits were to be stored and used only when needed. The men would sleep in hammocks. Lockers held the space suits and food. There was a bay for navigation instruments.

Behind the command module was a larger one, the service module, which held communications equipment and supplies of oxygen, water, and electrical power. Attached to it were four sets of small rockets that would be used to steer the service and command modules.

Finally there was a third module: the lunar module, which would be used for the lunar landing.

Because the capsules were so tremendously complex, countless tests of all types were run on them. Engineers checked and rechecked the physical spacecraft, while astronauts made numerous "dry runs," pretending to fly the *Apollo* into orbit while the command module simply sat on top of a tower.

It was during one of these many tests that a disaster occurred.

FIRE IN APOLLO

Encouraged by the string of Gemini successes—and prodded by two unmanned Soviet probes to the moon—NASA moved quickly with its Apollo preparations. The first manned Apollo flight was scheduled for February 1967 and would take two veteran astronauts and one rookie on a flight to test the new spacecraft in orbit.

Three weeks before the launch, on January 27, 1967,

an *Apollo* spacecraft sat in place on top of a *Saturn 1* booster rocket at the Kennedy Space Center to undergo routine tests. There were no plans for a lift-off; in fact, the *Saturn* rocket had no fuel in it. At 1:00 P.M. that day, three astronauts dressed in space suits entered the spacecraft to take it through a practice countdown and launch. First Virgil I. Grissom, who would sit in the seat farthest from the hatch, squirmed his way in. Spacewalker Edward H. White II followed, taking the middle seat. Finally Roger B. Chaffee, the youngest astronaut ever chosen to go into space, entered and sat in the seat next to the inside hatch.

Actually, there were three separate hatches on the spacecraft. There was an outer hatch, which was in the protective covering that shielded the spacecraft. After a launch it would drop off in space. Inside it was another hatch, built to withstand the intense heat of the spacecraft's reentry into the earth's atmosphere. The third hatch stayed in place, because air pressure from inside the spacecraft constantly pushed against it and kept it shut. The higher the pressure inside the cabin of the spacecraft, the more tightly shut was that hatch.

The spacecraft was to be run by inside batteries rather than by outside electricity.

Once inside, Grissom smelled an odor in his space suit oxygen supply. It was checked out, but nothing unusual was discovered.

After that nothing seemed wrong. The oxygen pressure in the cabin was raised to slightly higher than normal atmospheric pressure at sea level. The astronauts began practicing take-off routines and guiding the spacecraft into space. All moved ahead as planned with no hitches.

At 5:00 P.M. the astronauts in the spacecraft and personnel working in the blockhouse, located about 1,000 feet away, had some communications problems. Technicians nearby traced the problems to a defective microphone in the spacecraft. The crew could not turn it off.

Not long after, the trouble spread. Difficulties arose in the communication systems between the astronauts and the people standing by in the service tower.

At 6:30 P.M. there was a surge of power in the electrical system.

One minute later people heard a cry over the faulty communications system. To this day, no one knows exactly what the cry was—it could have been "Hey," or perhaps "Fire"—though several heard it.

Two seconds later, another sound came through. Once more, no one knows exactly what was said, but it seemed to be either "I've" or "we've."

Suddenly there was a clear message that all understood. "We've got a fire in the cockpit." The voice was probably Chaffee's.

Seven seconds went by. Then more messages. "They're fighting a bad fire. . . . Open 'er up. . . . We're burning up. . . . I'm getting out."

Then there was a cry of pain.

Engineer Donald Babbitt, the pad leader, immediately ordered, "Get 'em out of there." Then a burst of flame and smoke came out of the spacecraft. Babbitt felt himself thrown against a communications box by the explosion.

Above the workers on the service tower was a solid-fuel rocket attached to the spacecraft. If flames ignited it and it took off, it would destroy the tower and kill most people on it.

Babbitt's first thought was to flee for his life, but he raced toward the spacecraft instead. The scene there was like a nightmare. Men were grabbing what few gas masks they could. But the gas masks were not good enough to allow them to wade through the thick smoke pouring everywhere. Workers awkwardly tried to open the hatches with hatch tools, but the smoke kept overcoming them. One after another would back away and hand the tools over to someone else. One hatch, then another, was removed.

Finally the inner hatch was partly opened. To the people working on the hatches, it seemed as if an eternity passed, but in fact they had the hatches off at 6:36 P.M., only five minutes after a fire was reported. Babbitt went to the inner hatch and looked inside the cabin. He could barely make out the astronauts. Later he said that he was positive they were already dead.

The cause of death was listed as asphyxiation and inhalation of toxic fumes, mainly carbon monoxide. The astronauts had become unconscious in seconds.

So it was that NASA had its first fatalities.

Under instructions from the White House "to get to the bottom" of the accident, lengthy hearings were held among NASA officials and in Congress. The hearings determined the major causes of the accident to be faulty safety inspections; the use of pure oxygen, which allowed the flames to move so swiftly; the use of glycol, which is highly flammable; and faulty wiring, which chafed and set off a spark. The inner hatch was also listed as a problem, because once an unconscious astronaut fell against it, it could not be fully opened. There were other, but lesser, faults.

In retrospect, it was apparent that no one had even considered the possibility of a fire in the cockpit. The cockpit did not even have a fire extinguisher, and adequate firefighting equipment was nowhere near.

Accustomed to success after success, even during the most risky spaceflights, most people had great trouble accepting the death of the three astronauts. All mourned them and felt great sympathy for their families. Gus Grissom and Roger Chaffee were buried at Arlington National Cemetery. Edward White was buried at West Point.

For months, a dark cloud hung over NASA. The disaster made the public painfully aware of the risks involved with space exploration.

This first major NASA accident delayed the moon landings by several months as the timetable was scrapped and the entire Apollo system underwent a complete overhaul. The cabin was redesigned. Materials were made more fireproof, fire extinguishers were placed in the cabin, and pure oxygen was diluted with inert gases. The inner hatch was redesigned so that astronauts could open it from the inside in three seconds.

From February 26, 1966, to April 4, 1968, NASA sent six unmanned *Apollo* spacecrafts into suborbital and orbital flights.

On October 11, 1968, in *Apollo 7*, Walter M. Schirra, Donn F. Eisele, and R. Walter Cunningham orbited the earth for eleven days. The *Apollo* worked splendidly, and NASA decided the spacecraft was ready to go to the moon.

MEN CIRCLE THE MOON

On December 21, 1968, a new historic moment in the Space Age arrived. At Cape Canaveral a huge *Saturn 5* rocket pointed toward space. About 240,000 miles away was the moon. Atop the rocket sat the *Apollo 8* module, with Frank Borman, James Lovell, and William A. Anders inside. For the first time in the history of the human race, men would go to the moon. They would leave the earth's gravity and enter into the gravitational field of another celestial body. Most interesting, perhaps, they would be the first people *ever* to see the back side of the moon.

The largest, tensest, most excited crowd to date gathered to watch the lift-off. Flames spewed out and the heavily loaded rocket stood in a circle of flame without moving. Within minutes it was moving faster than any other man-carrying rocket had moved before.

As the *Apollo 8* left the earth, the three astronauts looked out of the windows and, for the first time ever, saw the planet Earth as a disk floating in black, empty space. Our planet seemed so small in infinite space. The men were simply awed. The photographs of the earth as it looked from space became among the most popular of the century.

Earth's gravity reaches out to an infinite distance. Of course, it becomes weaker and weaker the farther from Earth it is. When astronauts go to the moon, the pull of Earth's gravity weakens. At the same time, the pull of the moon's gravity becomes stronger. Where the moon's gravity has more effect than the earth's does, a rock dropped in space would fall toward the moon, not toward the earth.

When the astronauts entered the moon's gravitational field, the moon's gravity began to pull the spacecraft faster and faster toward the moon. They aimed retro-rockets toward the moon and fired them to slow down the spacecraft, and they were whipped around behind the moon.

When we look at the moon we see only one side of it. The same face of the moon is always pointed toward the earth. Until December 24, 1968, no one had seen the moon's dark side.

As the astronauts circled behind the moon at 4:49 A.M., December 24, NASA officials were nervous. The astronauts, however, were overwhelmed by what they saw. They looked down on a strange new world. The back of the moon is not so varied or mountainous as "our" face of the moon. It is monotonous, a vast plain dotted with countless craters, lonely beyond belief, and alien in an eerie way. Oddly, no one knows why the two faces differ so much.

While the astronauts were behind the moon, all radio and television communication stopped, because the moon blocked them. There was no way for NASA to be in touch with the astronauts. After what seemed a long wait, but was only twenty minutes, the signals began once more. The astronauts had come around again and were in orbit around the moon.

The next day, December 25, people all over the world were thrilled as they listened to a Christmas message sent from the moon to the earth by the astronauts. From space they read the biblical account of the creation of the earth and moon.

Then they headed back to Earth. The Apollo 8 mission was a major success.

Next, *Apollo 9*, with astronauts James McDivitt, David R. Scott, and Russell L. Schweickart, would go to the moon to test the moon lander.

While Scott orbited the moon in the command and service module, McDivitt and Schweickart flew away in the lunar module. The lunar module worked beautifully. McDivitt and Schweickart were able to pilot it to within miles of the moon's surface and then get back to connect up with the command module. Then all three astronauts returned safely to Earth.

Apollo 10 was the dress rehearsal for the real landing attempt. Its mission was to test the lunar module again and have it go almost, but not quite, to the moon's surface, and then return to the command module. The crew was made up of Thomas P. Stafford, John W. Young, and Eugene A. Cernan. On May 18, 1969, *Apollo 10* was launched and orbited the moon 31 times. Stafford and Cernan took the lunar module to within 47,000 feet of the surface—the closest that anyone had ever been to the moon. While near the end of its flight, the lunar module wobbled all over the place and almost went out of control, but Stafford gained control and once more went within nine miles of the moon's surface. The two astronauts returned to the *Apollo 10* command module and joined up with Young. The three returned to Earth.

Once again NASA had had a resounding success. All systems were go for the Apollo 11 mission, in which the astronauts would land on the moon and walk on its surface. The greatest moment in the history of space exploration was about to take place.

7

Men on the Moon

MEN ON THE MOON

We can divide human history into two periods. From the day the world began until 1969, no animal, no seed, no birds, and no human beings had ever left the earth to set foot on another world. All life on Earth had been bound to the planet by gravity. But that would change on July 16, 1969, when three men—Neil Armstrong, Michael Collins, and Edwin E. Aldrin—seated themselves in the *Apollo 11* capsule.

Vast numbers of nervous, happy, tense people gathered at Cape Canaveral to see the lift-off of the greatest exploration voyage in history. Tourists, politicians, foreign dignitaries, ambassadors, and military officials gathered to wait in the hot Florida sun. All listened anxiously to the countdown. The lift-off at 9:32 A.M. went smoothly, and the men were on their way to the moon. The trip, covered by television cameras aboard the spacecraft, was tense but uneventful.

As flight commander, Neil Armstrong would be most responsible for the forthcoming moon landing. It was he

The space vehicle for the *Apollo 11* lunar landing mission stands on the launchpad, about to take off and make its historic landing on the moon.

who would guide the tiny lunar module down to the surface of the moon.

Neil Armstrong

Neil Alden Armstrong was born on his grandparents' farm outside of Wapakoneta, Ohio, on August 5, 1930. As a child, he and his family lived in many different towns and cities.

Armstrong was an exceptionally active teenager. He joined a jazz combo and played the baritone horn. But above all he loved airplanes. At age fourteen he began taking flying lessons and received his pilot's license on his sixteenth birthday.

In 1947 Armstrong entered Purdue University to study aeronautical engineering as a Naval Air Cadet. After being at Purdue for two years he was called to active duty with the Navy. In Korea, he flew 78 combat missions, and he was shot down once, but survived. He won three Air Medals. Later he returned to Purdue, where he received a B.S. degree in 1955.

In seven years as a test pilot, Armstrong flew many advanced airplanes, pushing them as hard as he could. He tested the experimental X-15 airplane at speeds up to 4,000

Neil Armstrong, the first man ever to step on the moon. He, along with Michael Collins and Edwin E. Aldrin, went to the moon and back in the *Apollo 11* spacecraft, July 16–24, 1969.

miles per hour and at altitudes of forty miles above the earth. He was considered to be an excellent pilot by all who knew him. One person remarked that he flew airplanes as though he wore them.

Armstrong worked for the National Advisory Committee for Aeronautics, which later became NASA. It was natural that he would someday become an astronaut.

As an astronaut, Armstrong proved he could survive almost anything. On March 16, 1966, he was the command pilot of *Gemini 8*. With him was David Scott. Armstrong guided the spacecraft in the first manual space docking, trying to connect it with an *Agenda* rocket. As they connected, a small rocket on the *Gemini 8* stopped functioning properly. Suddenly the *Gemini 8* and *Agenda* rocket went into a wild spin. Armstrong backed the spinning spacecraft away from the *Agenda* rocket; then firing 16 different small rockets, he stopped the spacecraft from spinning. NASA officials, who realized that few could have survived that accident, praised Armstrong for his "extraordinary piloting skill."

A little over two years later, Armstrong had to escape from a jet moon-landing trainer. He parachuted from a height of 200 feet and lived. Seldom is there time to get a parachute open on such a low jump. But Armstrong managed it.

NASA was impressed. They felt sure that if anyone could pilot the first moon lander to the moon, it was Armstrong.

On the way to the moon, Armstrong, Aldrin, and Collins had time to wonder about the days ahead of them. Their landing would be far more dangerous than any ever undertaken by the explorers of old.

Hour by hour they got closer to the moon. On July 19 their spacecraft began to orbit the moon. Armstrong and

Aldrin later entered the lunar landing module, *Eagle*. At 4:05 P.M. Eastern Daylight Time, they fired rockets on the *Eagle* and left the command module with Collins in it behind them. They slowly began descending toward the surface of the moon.

The lunar module was incredibly fragile. Because it would be used in airless space, it was not streamlined like an airplane. Its long, thin legs made it look like a spider.

Armstrong piloted the delicate lunar module toward a landing spot chosen long before, the Sea of Tranquillity. (If you look at the full moon some night, you can see the Sea of Tranquillity. It is a dark, flat area near the very center of the moon, but a little to the right and above. Astronomers long ago thought that such regions were literally seas, but they are merely flat areas.)

As Armstrong and Aldrin approached the landing spot, the whole world heard Armstrong speaking to the NASA officials in Houston, Texas. Nearing the landing area, he was startled by the appearance of huge boulders. If the lunar module were to hit one it would be smashed into a dozen pieces.

Armstrong turned on some rocket engines, and the lunar module lifted a bit. With difficulty, he flew over and just missed the boulders. Because the moon lander was low on fuel, Armstrong wondered whether it would be safer to go back to Collins's ship in orbit and forget about landing. The moon landing could wait; other astronauts could try it later. He decided to go ahead. Officials on Earth, who knew exactly what was happening, were extremely anxious. The tension rose.

Then Armstrong announced, in a voice heard all over the world, "The Eagle has landed." It was 4:14 P.M., July 19, 1969.

The astronauts had made a safe landing. Eight years after President Kennedy had announced the almost unbelievable national goal, men were actually on the moon.

After landing the lunar module, Armstrong and Aldrin spent another six and a half hours inside. To prepare for their first walk on the moon, they had to put on their space suits and life-support packs—not an easy thing to do. Each had to help the other get dressed and prepared. Finally they were ready to descend.

For weeks before the moon landing, everyone wondered what the first man on the moon might say. Some joked that it would be "Oops, I just stepped in chewing gum," or "Look at that huge footprint over there." Others expected something very solemn or patriotic.

Finally the great moment arrived. Armstrong and Aldrin got the hatch door open and lowered the ladder. Then Armstrong, moving very carefully so that he would not fall or rip his space suit (which could have been fatal), slowly descended the ladder. When his foot touched the surface

Edwin Aldrin descends the lunar module ladder to join Neil Armstrong in the first moon walk.

of the moon, Armstrong said, "That is one small step for man, one giant leap for mankind."

It was 10:56 P.M. Eastern Daylight Time, July 20, 1969.

For those watching and listening, it all seemed impossible. Many watching had been born before the first automobiles had been invented, before radios had been invented, before the Wright Brothers flew an airplane.

A few minutes after Armstrong stepped on the moon, Aldrin joined him. Aldrin looked about him at the vast plain dotted with countless craters and called it "a magnificent desolation."

The astronauts brought some personal items with them. Armstrong brought some jewelry that belonged to the women in his family and planned to bring the objects back to them as mementos of his moon walk. Aldrin brought a chalice and a tiny flask of wine so that he could take Holy Communion in the lunar module.

They also brought an American flag, which they put up with some difficulty, for it was not easy to push the flagpole into the hard ground. Since there is no air or wind on the moon, a wire held the flag out so that it could be seen. The astronauts posed next to the flag for the automatic camera to take pictures.

They also brought medals for the astronauts who had died, and, at the request of the Soviet government, Russian medals in honor of cosmonauts Yuri Gagarin and Vladimir Komarov, who had died. The medals were left on the moon.

There were many tasks for Armstrong and Aldrin to complete on the first moon landing. First, they brought out a sheet of aluminum foil and attached it upright on a staff, aimed toward the sun. The sun continually sends charged particles toward the moon, Earth, and other planets and satellites of the solar system. The earth's atmosphere blocks most of the particles. Would the moon's thin atmosphere—if it had any—block them, too? If it had no

Edwin Aldrin stands next to the American flag that he and Neil Armstrong planted on the moon's surface.

atmosphere, what sort of particles would constantly strike it? Whatever type of particles hit the moon during the astronauts' stay would be captured on the foil. The astronauts planned to roll up the foil just before leaving and bring it back to Earth for scientists to examine.

They also put out a 4-pound (moon weight) seismometer. It consisted of a cylinder 15 inches high and 11 inches in diameter. Inside was a suspended weight. If the moon happened to jiggle from a moonquake, a radio attached to the cylinder would send information to Earth about its frequency and intensity.

Scientists eagerly awaited this experiment, designed to show how active the moon is. Frequent moonquakes would indicate molten lava under the surface, or a shifting crust like the earth's, or collision with a large meteorite.

From such a small instrument, much could be learned. The seismometer batteries were designed to last two years. It and the seismometer left by the next Apollo crews showed that the moon is mostly a dead planet lacking crustal movement or the eruption of volcanoes.

The astronauts also left a laser mirror, which weighed 11 pounds on the moon (a full 66 pounds on Earth). It had 100 reflecting prisms in it and resembled a large highway sign reflector. It was aimed toward the earth. Later, laser beams would be sent from Cloudcroft Air Force Base, New Mexico, and from Hawaii to hit the reflector and return to Earth. That way scientists could determine the exact distance between Earth and moon.

One might wonder why scientists needed such accurate measurements. There has been reason to believe that the moon is drifting away from the earth at a very slow pace. This drift can be measured over a period of many years. It is also known that the earth wobbles on its axis a little each year. The wobble is always slightly different. Wind patterns, new winter snows, moving glaciers, and changing water levels in lakes cause weight shifts on the earth's surface, pulling the earth this way and that each year. The earth's wobble was known, though it had not been accurately measured, but no one knew if the moon wobbled. Furthermore, the earth and moon attract each other. Did the gravity field between them vary? The simple reflectors would help answer these questions.

What scientists wanted most of all were moon rocks. The moon's geology was almost a complete mystery.

As the astronauts went about collecting 50 pounds of rocks, they discussed with Houston the dirt and rocks and landscape they saw. Hopping here and there in the low gravity like kangaroos, they delighted everyone watching them on television back on Earth. At one point Armstrong said to Aldrin, "This is fun, isn't it?"

While Armstrong and Aldrin bounded about on the

The first astronaut team of seven. Front row, left to right: Walter M. Shirra, Jr.; Donald K. Slayton; John H. Glenn, Jr.; and Malcolm (Scott) Carpenter. Back row, left to right: Alan B. Shepard, Jr.; Virgil I. (Gus) Grissom; and Leroy (Gordon) Cooper.

The *Gemini VII* spacecraft in orbit at an altitude of 160 miles on December 15, 1965. The picture was taken through the hatch window of the nearby *Gemini VI* during rendezvous maneuvers.

Astronaut Edward H. White II on his historic space walk. Attached to two lines, White moved around for 21 minutes with the help of a hand-held maneuvering unit.

Recovery of the first unmanned *Apollo*. Note how the heat and flames of its reentry into the atmosphere have charred the spacecraft.

Astronaut Edwin E. Aldrin, Jr., the pilot of the lunar module, walks on the moon during the Apollo 11 mission. Aldrin was the second man to step on the moon, minutes after Neil Armstrong.

Apollo 11 astronauts saw this view of the earth rising over the horizon of the moon as they made their lunar orbit.

A composite photograph of the sun, taken from Skylab. A huge eruption can be seen on the top of the sun. It reaches 500,000 miles out into space. (The distance of the moon from Earth is only half that far.)

Opposite, top: The Great Red Spot of Jupiter. Six Earths could fit in the red spot, from top to bottom. From Earth, even with the best telescopes, the red spot is difficult to see.

Opposite, bottom: The planet Saturn, taken from *Voyager 2* from a distance of 27 million miles.

The first space shuttle launch, April 12, 1981.

The space shuttle *Challenger* accident of
January 28, 1986, at 11:39:16 A.M. Eastern Standard
Time. A booster rocket, ripped loose, flies away by
itself. Part of the shuttle wreckage can be seen in
the cloud.

moon, in full view, Michael Collins circled the moon for hours all by himself. When his spacecraft took him around to the other side of the moon, Collins was completely out of contact with any other human being.

After their moon walk, Armstrong and Aldrin got into the top half of the lunar module. The most dangerous part of their trip had arrived. If all did not go 100 percent correctly, they would be marooned on the moon to die in a few hours. There was no way for them to be rescued.

They fired the necessary explosives to break the bolts that held the ascent stage to the lower half of the lunar module. Free of the lower half, the pilot ignited the engine of the main rocket. Officials at NASA waited nervously. But the takeoff was smooth. They guided the lunar module to the rendezvous spot, met the orbiting *Apollo* command module, and hooked together. Armstrong and Aldrin crawled into the command module to rejoin Collins.

The lunar module was fired so that it would crash into the moon. The crash of the lunar module sent small shock waves through the rocks of the moon, causing tiny moon-quakes, which the seismometer recorded for the benefit of earthbound geologists.

In the meantime, rockets were fired on the command module, and the astronauts, with a valuable cargo of moon rocks, headed back to Earth.

After landing safely in the Pacific Ocean, the astronauts were immediately put into quarantine for seventeen days in case they might have picked up some terrible diseases from the moon. The astronauts were placed in a small sealed van. President Richard M. Nixon went to visit them. Obviously pleased, he stood outside, waving and smiling at them through a sealed window.

The United States had done what Kennedy had promised it would do—put men on the moon before the decade was out. On Kennedy's grave at Arlington Cemetery, someone placed a message: "Mr. President, the Eagle has landed."

TO GO TO THE MOON AGAIN?

President Nixon, thrilled by America's triumph, met in secret with his top advisers and NASA officials. What next? Should NASA keep sending men to the moon? Was it worth the huge cost, the great risk? What if a rocket blew up, or an accident took place out in space? Nixon and his advisers knew the terrible danger of space travel. Americans had been killed on the ground and nearly died in space. The Soviet Union had lost Cosmonaut Komarov in an accident in space. Why take further risks? Why tarnish the success of NASA with a possible failure?

Nixon's advisers and NASA officials pushed to continue the moon landings. NASA had the equipment and the know-how, they argued. It would look bad in the eyes of the world to turn around after one success. Most important, there were good scientific reasons for going to the moon again. The geology of the moon was still a puzzle. Analysis of the rocks Aldrin and Armstrong brought back showed that they contained minerals never before seen, new to science. Whatever they could find out about the moon would help them understand the geology of the earth better.

By the end of the meeting, it was agreed that the moon landings would continue.

MORE MOON TRIPS

On a trip lasting from November 14 to November 24, 1969, Charles Conrad, Richard F. Gordon, and Alan L. Bean went to the moon. Conrad and Bean landed with pinpoint precision on the Ocean of Storms (just to the left of center on the full moon) on November 19 and explored the area near their lunar module.

Conrad knew that the second trip to the moon would not make history. The world would not listen to his every word as they did with Armstrong. When Conrad, who is short, came down the ladder to step onto the moon, he said, "Whoopee, man. That may have been one small step for Neil, but that's a long one for me."

Conrad and Bean walked over to the old *Surveyor*, an unmanned spacecraft that had landed on the moon to photograph it two years earlier. They cut away some of its metal to bring back to Earth, so scientists could see how metals stood up to the harsh conditions of space. They also set up a small observatory that would automatically send back information about magnetism and other geophysical matters. And the two astronauts collected more rocks. As they worked they clearly enjoyed themselves, often joking and laughing.

After staying on the moon for 31.5 hours—three times as long as Armstrong and Aldrin had spent—they joined up with the *Apollo 12* command module and with Gordon headed back to Earth for a safe landing.

NASA's triumphs grew. Again and again, trips into space turned out well.

Then came the trip of *Apollo 13.* James A. Lovell, John L. Swigert, and Fred W. Haise took off for a moon landing on April 11, 1970. As the command module neared the moon, the astronauts heard a loud explosion.

Right away, NASA officials in Houston realized that an oxygen tank had burst. Without oxygen, the astronauts would soon die in space. Engineers and scientists in Houston quickly went into action. What, if anything, could be done to save the astronauts? At first, it seemed the astronauts faced certain death. Fortunately, the astronauts had not yet landed on the moon. They still had the lunar module, which, though small, did have its own oxygen supply. NASA officials instructed the astronauts circling the moon to use whatever supplies they could from the lunar module. They were also to fly back to Earth with it still attached to the command module. If all went well and they had no more problems, perhaps they might get back to Earth alive.

For a few tense days, the world waited. Newspapers followed the story of the stranded astronauts. Everywhere bulletins flashed on the news broadcasts.

With the last of the oxygen nearly used up, the astronauts landed safely on the waves of the Pacific Ocean. The near-disaster actually became yet another NASA victory. NASA engineers, scientists, and astronauts never looked better.

After *Apollo 13*, there were more moon landings, all of them highly successful and free of problems. Alan B. Shepard, Stuart A. Roosa, and Edgar D. Mitchell went to the moon on the Apollo 14 mission, from January 31 to February 9, 1971. They landed in the Fra Mauro region of the moon, a rather rugged highlands area just a bit to the left of the very center of the full moon.

Shepard and Mitchell were the first astronauts to use a vehicle on the moon. They pulled a wheeled contraption, much like a rickshaw, with them and loaded it with valuable moon rocks.

The *Apollo 17* lunar lander is visible just behind a lunar rover. Astronauts Harrison H. Schmitt and Eugene A. Cernan explored the moon for 75 hours.

Lunar module pilot Harrison H. Schmitt stands on the moon next to a huge boulder during the Apollo 17 mission. The background shows the mountainous landscape of the Taurus-Littrow landing site.

David R. Scott, Alfred M. Worden, and James B. Irwin were on the Apollo 15 mission, from July 26 to August 7, 1971. They landed next to the famous and remarkable Hadley Rill, a very large canyon apparent above the center of the full moon. They were the first astronauts to use a lunar roving vehicle self-powered by electric batteries.

John W. Young, Thomas K. Mattingly, and Charles M. Duke of the Apollo 16 mission, April 16 to April 27, 1972, landed in the rugged Descartes Highlands (below and to the right of the center of the full moon). This was the first time that astronauts had landed in a mountainous region of the moon. Scientists were quite sure that the rocks from highland areas would be different from those found on the plains, and they were right. The astronauts discovered crystalline rocks of a type never seen before. They also collected a white soil not previously encountered.

These astronauts were the first to take to the moon a small astronomical observatory, which contained a telescope that saw ultraviolet light. On Earth we cannot see the ultraviolet light of distant stars, nor of a hydrogen cloud that surrounds the earth. They photographed the earth, showing the cloud of hydrogen. They also photographed new features of the Milky Way.

The astronauts drove up into the mountains and were the first ever to be on high moon peaks.

Eugene A. Cernan, Ronald E. Evans, and Harrison H. Schmitt of the Apollo 17 mission, December 7 to December 19, 1972, landed near the Crater Littrow, which rises near the Sea of Serenity. This landing site is to the right of and above the center of the full moon. Of all the landing sites, it is the farthest from the center.

Until *Apollo 17*, the majority of the scientific experiments duplicated each other. The repetition allowed scientists to compare them and to see if the moon varied from locale to locale. Since the Apollo 17 mission would be the last, scientists decided to send a new set of experiments.

In one, the astronauts set off charges of high explosives. Energy waves sank beneath the surface, moving much like sound waves and bouncing off lower rocks. The echoes could be picked up on the surface and precisely timed. These returning waves made patterns on a film, showing scientists structures far below the surface of the moon.

Meanwhile, radio waves were sent from the orbiter, which flew around the moon high overhead. These radio waves also penetrated the surface of the moon to a depth of three-quarters of a mile and returned to the orbiter. They, too, revealed rocks beneath the surface.

The astronauts drilled eight-foot holes into the surface and brought back cores of rocks.

Several experiments were made to determine the precise gravity of the moon at different places. Heavy underground rocks, made of massive materials such as iron, would change the gravity readings. No iron was found, but there were gravity changes.

The astronauts discovered orange rocks that surprised geologists by proving to be extremely old, far older than Earth rocks.

Before they left the moon, the astronauts unveiled a plaque dedicated to peace.

Apollo 17 was the last lunar mission for the time being. At this date, no one knows exactly when another astronaut or cosmonaut, Russian or American, man or woman, will go to the moon.

WHAT WAS DISCOVERED ON THE MOON?

One thing that greatly puzzled scientists was the age of the moon. Was it older or younger than the earth? Another was the moon's surface. Were the craters volcanic? Or were they all formed by meteorites and comets that smashed into the moon long ago?

And, of course, was there life on the moon?

The best telescope on Earth gave no answers to these questions, but rocks brought back from the Apollo missions did go a long way toward answering many of these and other questions.

First of all, some rocks found on the moon by the astronauts are far older than any found on Earth. This does not actually mean that the moon is older than the earth. Most rocks on Earth have been reformed and changed many times over. We will probably never find the rocks that were on Earth when the earth began. Even so, the moon rocks strongly suggest that the moon is older than the earth.

The moon rocks did not in themselves fully explain the moon's formation. In late 1986, however, scientists developed a new theory: Apparently, over a billion years ago a large celestial body about the size of the moon hit the earth dead center. The force was tremendous. Heavy metals that had gravitated to the center of the earth when it was young and molten spewed into space. Huge chunks of the earth broke away and flew into space as well. The heat of the impact was so great that the rocks lost all their water; steam vapor simply drifted off. The chunks collected together and formed our moon.

If this theory is accurate, it explains many things about the geology of the earth and moon that were not understood before. The impact of the celestial body on the earth, for instance, explains the mystery of why there are heavy metals such as lead and gold found near the surface of the earth. And the theory explains the complete absence of any trace of water on the moon or in the rocks brought back by the astronauts.

So parts of the moon were probably once part of the earth. When it was first formed, it must have been molten. Moonquakes detected by seismometers left on the moon show that deep down there are still some molten areas. They probably remain liquid because they are heated by radioactive elements. When underground pockets of the liquid magma move, small quakes shake the moon.

One important moon feature remains to be explained: the craters. They are everywhere, some miles in diameter, others only inches across. How were they formed?

The vast majority of them were formed by meteorites, although a number of them are volcanic. After the newly formed molten moon cooled and hardened, it encountered a meteorite shower about 4 billion years ago. Meteorites kept smashing into the moon, creating almost all of the craters. Somewhere between 3.9 and 3.3 billion years ago, lava from volcanoes flowed from craters and fissures on the side of the moon facing the earth. This lava flowed into low-lying regions to form the "oceans," which of course are not oceans at all but flat plains. By the time the lava cooled to form solid rock, the meteorite bombardments had ceased. Very rarely since then have large meteorites hit these "oceans."

For the last 3.3 billion years little has taken place on the moon. Some minor changes occur when the sun shoots out particles that travel almost at the speed of light, hitting the moon and pulverizing grains of rock. Over billions of years, these particles have slowly formed lunar dust and soil. But what we see today is essentially an unchanged moon, whose surface is 3.3 billion years old.

The moon is almost, but not quite, a dead body. Hundreds of centuries may go by before a single happening takes place. A few gases from hot areas of the interior may escape, and clouds rise up. Magma deep in the moon occasionally moves, sending moonquakes to the surface. Every now and then, a meteorite hits the moon. (Monks in the Middle Ages reported seeing a fiery light on the moon, probably the result of a meteorite hit.)

And in the future? It is likely that the moon will look almost exactly the same 3 billion years from now as it does today. In comparison, the earth will look radically different. Not a single mountain range we see today will still exist. The continents will have shifted so much we wouldn't recognize them. Interestingly, the only thing future human beings will see billions of years from now that we see today will be the same old features of the moon.

8

Apollo-Soyuz

The history of space exploration shows mostly competition between the two superpowers. Yet at times they have cooperated, sharing information and, on one historic occasion, conducting a joint mission.

In 1962 President Kennedy exchanged letters with Premier Khrushchev, spelling out cooperation in space, especially in the fields of biomedicine and meteorology.

On October 10, 1969, the NASA administrator opened new discussions with the president of the Soviet Academy of Sciences to explore the possibility of a joint USA-USSR space venture. Of most interest was the idea of an American and a Russian spacecraft meeting in space while in orbit. Such a rendezvous would show that American and Soviet equipment could be used together for future space exploration. For the present it would show that the Americans and Russians could rescue each other in case of an emergency.

These discussions were held against a background of improved American and Russian relations. There was a "thaw" in the cold war. President Nixon was working successfully toward a détente with the Soviets, who had their own political and economic reasons for cooperating.

NASA saw a joint venture with the USSR as an opportunity to learn more about the Russian space efforts. The Russians had made several "firsts" in space. But little was known about Soviet space technology. Soviet computers remained a mystery. NASA wondered how cosmonauts guided manned spaceships and how Soviets docked their spacecraft in space.

In 1970 American space officials went to Moscow to meet with Russian officials. There, at a Soviet space center in Kazakhstan, they saw firsthand the Soviet launchers and

This illustration by David Meltzer shows the United States' *Apollo* spacecraft docking with the Soviet Union's *Soyuz*.

spacecraft. The American engineers were amazed. The main Soviet manned spacecraft, the *Soyuz*, was by American standards unbelievably crude. It had *never* been designed as a manned spacecraft, as *Gemini*, *Mercury*, and *Apollo* had been, but had been converted from an unmanned spacecraft to hold cosmonauts. In sharp contrast to the American astronauts, the Soviet cosmonauts had hardly any control over their own flights. They could not guide the craft as it returned to the earth's atmosphere. Instead the craft spun to keep on track, much as a rifle bullet is spun for the same reason. This produced terrible nausea. While in orbit, cosmonauts kept their spacecraft in the correct position by looking at the earth's horizon with a periscope. When on the night side of the earth, they had no way of controlling the spacecraft.

The Americans were stunned to find that the *Soyuz* had no on-board computer. American spacecraft had pow-

Cosmonauts Valeriy N. Kubasov, engineer of the Soviet crew (on the left), and commander Aleksey A. Leonov (on the right), in the orbital module during the US-USSR docking of the *Apollo* and *Soyuz* in space. Note the American and Russian flags sewn on the sleeves of the cosmonauts.

erful computers, the world's best, on board. Americans controlled their spacecraft through a computer network, and astronauts could use their computer in emergencies to plan and carry out new and original procedures if necessary. Remarkably, the information for controls on board the *Soyuz* was on a roll of cardboard with punched-out holes. Instead of computers timing and operating jet blasts to change course, the cosmonauts did this work by the crude method of looking at jet nozzles through a periscope and timing the blasts with a stopwatch.

In the eyes of the Americans, the Soviets worked with primitive equipment. Yet with it the Soviets had accomplished a great deal. The brave cosmonauts had overcome many limitations to explore space.

Before any docking procedures could be worked out, the Americans and Soviets had to solve many technical problems. One was the fact that the docking system of the *Soyuz* and *Apollo* were very different. More advanced, the *Soyuz* docking system worked automatically. The Americans docked mainly by eyeball, the pilot watching and easing the spacecraft together.

The Americans decided that they would dock by sight with the *Soyuz*, and the Soviets agreed. But the *Soyuz*, painted a dull color, was difficult to see. If it were painted any lighter in color the *Soyuz* would become too cold in space, and if it were painted darker it would be too hot inside. (The cooling system of a spacecraft depends upon its color, which either absorbs the sun's rays if dark, or reflects them if light.) The Soviets equipped the *Soyuz* with beacons and bright blinking lights, so that the Americans could find it out in space.

Another technical problem was the air pressure in the two spacecraft. The Soviets could not go from the *Soyuz* into the *Apollo* without getting a dreadful illness called the bends. (Workers in tunnels or sea divers can get the bends if they go suddenly from a high pressure atmosphere to a low pressure atmosphere. Gas bubbles appear in the blood and can produce severe pain and cause paralysis.) The pressure of the two spacecraft had to be equalized so that the men could go from one to the other.

While the Americans were in the Soviet Union, they swapped space stories with the Russians and found out a great deal about the cosmonauts' personal experiences in space. For example, Yuriy Romanenko and Georgiy Grechko had a tense moment during a space walk. Grechko went out for his space walk, attached to the spacecraft by a rope. Romanenko, wanting to watch him, leaned too far out of the spacecraft. As Grechko admired the view, he suddenly saw Romanenko floating by. Just in the nick of time, Grechko grabbed his fellow cosmonaut and the two got back into their spacecraft. If Grechko had not gotten to him, Romanenko would stilll be floating in space.

During his trip to Moscow in May 1972, Nixon spoke of the coming space rendezvous with Premier Aleksey Kosygin. During a time when both countries were actively seeking better relations, they signed a five-year agreement allowing the space rendezvous to take place.

Over the next three years Soviet and American astronauts and cosmonauts traveled back and forth between the two countries many times, making preparations for the historic meeting, called the Apollo-Soyuz Test Project (ASTP). On July 15, 1975, the *Soyuz 19* spacecraft was launched from the Baikonur cosmodrome in Kazakhstan. Seven and a half hours later, an *Apollo* spacecraft was launched from Cape Canaveral. On July 17 the two spacecraft approached each other and were joined together.

The American astronauts were Thomas P. Stafford, Donald K. Slayton, and Vance D. Brand. The cosmonauts were Aleksey A. Leonov and Valeriy N. Kubasov. The astronauts and cosmonauts got along very well together and greatly enjoyed the trip. They shared some soup from a container that they had pasted over with a label "vodka."

Television cameras on board allowed people all over the world to see the men in orbit together. What the world saw was, in a sense, an anticlimax. The real adventure had taken place during long bull sessions between astronauts, cosmonauts, and engineers. A great deal was learned, and both the Americans and Russians found much to admire in each other's efforts.

The ASTP in its own way laid the foundation for future American and Russian ventures. Both countries expect to cooperate in any manned exploration of Mars. Other nations may very well join in with them. Partially because of the costs of such extraordinarily expensive ventures and also for political reasons, we will almost certainly see greater international cooperation in space in the future.

9

The Planets

From earliest times, people all over the world have noticed that certain "stars" in the sky wandered about, changing position from month to month, year to year. The Greeks called them "planets," which simply meant wanderers.

Until the 1960s, astronomers had a limited amount of information about the planets—only what telescopes and mathematical equations could reveal. For everything that was known, vast amounts remained unknown.

The space advances of the 1960s demonstrated to NASA (and to the Soviet Union) that rockets and small unmanned space probes could be sent to the distant planets. The cost of space probes would not be high compared to the expense of manufacturing and manning telescopes and the hundreds of millions of dollars a year spent for astronomers of all nations to gather information about the planets. Some of the funds given to NASA by Congress and approved by the president were for the exploration of the planets, even during the times when the moon race was a top priority.

There were countless questions astronomers wished to answer. Each government spends tens, even hundreds of millions of dollars gathering and analyzing weather information and making daily and weekly forecasts. Astronomers and meteorologists could benefit greatly if they knew how planetary atmosphere, in general, operated. The more they could find out about how planetary weather systems worked, the more solid knowledge they would have to make more accurate weather forecasts here on Earth. Atmospheric studies could also help us learn what gases heat up planets and help explain long-term climate changes like the earth's Ice Age.

Space probes to distant planets could also help geologists know how and when the earth was formed. Did the earth start out cold and later heat up? Or was it hot and molten, later cooling down? If it was originally molten, minerals would have been distributed so that the heaviest, such as gold and lead, would lie mostly very deep in the earth. If it was always cool (and especially cooler than now), minerals would be distributed differently. This is a geologic puzzle of great economic importance. Its answer will help geologists locate vital minerals. Another puzzle concerns oil. Did all crude oil on Earth come from living organisms? Or is it a natural mineral? The discovery of oil on other planets could answer this question once and for all.

Could life exist on distant planets? Did Mars once have life, even if it has none today? Are there organic compounds on planets that might form life a few million years in the future? Do conditions on other planets make it possible to set up space colonies?

Few areas of science are as mysterious as the planets. The responsibility for U.S. efforts in exploring the planets fell mostly on the shoulders of the people at the Jet Propulsion Laboratory in Pasadena, California, along with their worldwide network of radio antennae, which would pick up spacecraft signals from the probes. Space probes designed and manufactured at the JPL would be placed on rockets and fired, usually from Cape Canaveral.

Space travel offered us the opportunity to explore and to expand our knowledge of the planets. Space probes would send back to Earth extraordinary new information. We had no idea what would or could be discovered.

MERCURY

Astronomers and geologists were particularly interested in Mercury. If its geology turned out to be like Earth's, then it was likely that many planets originated at the same time and under similar conditions. If not, then new ideas about the formation of the planets would be considered. The rotation of the planet was unknown, as was the surface temperature. To know Mercury's temperature would help scientists determine both the heat output of the sun and the amount of the sun's heat received by the earth's upper atmosphere.

NASA realized that a trip to Mercury would be exceptionally tricky. The best route from Earth to Mercury called for a terribly long journey, no less than 250 million miles. But that was the least of it. Any spacecraft that had to operate near Mercury, so close to the sun, could be easily damaged by the heat. It would encounter searing temperatures of as high as 415°C (779°F) in the sunlight—hot enough to melt tin and lead. Few cameras, scanners, or electrical parts can operate in such temperature. Worse still, the shadowed areas would be 175°C below zero (-283°F). Very special equipment had to be designed to operate over such a huge temperature range.

NASA met the test. The agency designed a promising spacecraft named *Mariner*. *Mariner* probes went to Venus, Mars, and Mercury.

It was the voyage of *Mariner 10* that made history—but just barely. After being launched on November 3, 1973, *Mariner 10* suffered one problem after another during its long flight of nearly four months. Several times, officials at

A *Mariner 10* spacecraft photograph of the planet Mercury, taken March 29, 1974. Note how the planet resembles our moon with its craters and barren, lifeless landscape.

NASA were sure it would fail when it got near Mercury—if it ever got there at all.

After flying for 146 days through 250 million miles of space, *Mariner 10* neared Mercury. Amazingly, it was only 104 miles off course—a bull's-eye. After photographing Mercury on March 29, 1974, *Mariner 10* circled the sun and met up with Mercury again on September 21, 1974. Then *Mariner* photographed Mercury, circled the sun, and returned to photograph the planet once more on March 16, 1975.

Its delicate cameras were protected by a metal parasol. Solar panels that looked like venetian blinds turned sunlight into electrical energy to power the equipment on board. Pictures were taken and information sent back to

Earth at the speed of light. Even so, it took about ten minutes for the signals to reach Earth. *Mariner* revealed many secrets of the hidden planet and went on forever into space.

Mercury is a terrifyingly barren world, which in many ways resembles our moon. Everywhere there are craters. Long breaks in the planet's surface show up as escarpments, or cliffs of the type formed by earthquakes.

Most amazing of all is a huge crater, now called Caloris Plantia (also called Caloris Basin). The impact of the meteor that made the crater was so great that shock waves went right through the planet to form rugged mountains on the opposite side.

There is no atmosphere. All is either tremendously hot or cold. Sunlight on Mercury is like having five noonday suns here.

The motion of Mercury is strange almost beyond belief. It takes Mercury longer to spin one revolution on its axis than to orbit the sun once. In other words, its "day" lasts longer than its "year." As seen from Mercury, the sun can rise in the west, move in one direction, pause, move backward for weeks in the sky, and then go forward again.

The *Mariner* flight sent back exceptionally clear pictures of this unusual planet. Scientists will continue to study them for decades to come.

The importance of Mercury lies in the fact that no erosion has taken place on it—it is a planet untouched by wind or rains. We see it just as it looked billions of years ago. Because Mercury and Earth were formed at approximately the same time and more or less from the same materials, we are able to see what our planet looked like when it was first formed.

By knowing the early geology of the earth we can better understand how today's geology came about, how mountains were formed and minerals deposited, and much more.

VENUS

Venus, the morning and evening "star," is the brightest celestial object we ever see aside from the sun and moon. Its light is so great that it can sometimes cast tree shadows on snow. In its size and location in the solar system, it is the planet most like Earth, but it is closer to the sun.

Since the invention of good telescopes in the 1600s, scientists have known that Venus is covered with very dense clouds, which they naturally thought held rain. They believed Venus was a damp place covered with oceans and steamy swamps. Many astronomers imagined that the planet was a "Garden of Eden"—a lush, warm, paradise. Once we entered the Space Age, scientists all over the world looked forward to the day that spacecraft would go to Venus and attempt to discover what this mysterious planet is really like.

The Soviet Union was the first nation to send spacecraft to Venus. From February 12, 1961, to June 14, 1975, they sent several probes, which showed that Venus was a startling place—unlike anything anyone could have imagined. There were thick clouds all right, but they were not rain clouds. In fact, they were mostly clouds of sulfuric acid— a powerful acid that can eat through clothing and burn one's skin. The land beneath the clouds was more barren, more scorched, and far drier than the worst desert on Earth. Ground temperatures reached 900°F.

NASA, too, sent several probes to Venus. The first, *Mariner 1*, failed in a launch attempt, but *Mariner 2* was successfully launched on August 27, 1962. It flew past Venus and radioed back important information about the planet's magnetism and temperature readings. *Mariner 5* also flew by Venus and sent back similar information. Since then, many American and especially Russian spacecraft have gone into orbit around Venus and photographed the clouds for days at a time. American spacecraft also mapped the ground beneath the clouds by using radar equipment. Radar signals can go right through clouds, hit the ground, bounce back, and go through the clouds again to be recorded by a spacecraft.

At about the same time, the Soviet Union landed several more craft, which succeeded in obtaining some photographs of the surface of Venus. They show an exceptionally bleak landscape. The ground is covered with rocks that appear to be broken. Because the atmosphere is so much thicker than the earth's, it curves light rays, just as thick glass does. So, instead of being flat as on Earth, the horizon is seen to have a U shape.

Because of the extensive Soviet and American efforts, we know a good deal about Venus. Perhaps of greatest interest to scientists is the knowledge of how the clouds move. It is impossible to make a model of the earth's atmosphere with which to conduct experiments. But the atmospheres on other planets—Venus, Mars, Jupiter, and Saturn—serve as models. By studying them scientists see how heat is transferred, how winds gather speed, how the upper layers mix with lower layers, and so on. In short, the atmospheres of other planets give us a better understanding of how our own atmosphere works.

The radar-produced maps of the ground and Russian photographs show that the geology of Venus is basically like that of Earth. Deep underground forces similar to those on Earth have broken the crustal rocks of Venus and pushed up mountain ranges. There are great differences as well. Our own landscapes are shaped mostly by erosion from running water, glaciers, and sometimes windblown sand. Venusian erosion is different because there is no water or ice on that planet—no rivers to carve valleys, no glaciers to shape mountaintops.

In the future, Venus will be studied in far greater detail. There is much to learn about our weather conditions by studying weather conditions on Venus.

MARS

Of all the unexplored planets, none has intrigued people so much as Mars. When good telescopes became available, astronomers realized that Mars had an atmosphere, as well as two polar caps. The caps changed size, indicating that some sort of ice was up there that melted in the Martian summertime, and formed during Martian winters. The planet changed colors with the seasons, which seemed to indicate that plants lived on Mars. This gave rise to theories about possible intelligent life on Mars, and hundreds of stories were written about Martians.

Once we entered the Space Age, people eagerly looked forward to the exploration of Mars by spacecraft.

NASA launched *Mariner 3* (the same sort of spacecraft that had already gone to Venus and would later go to Mer-

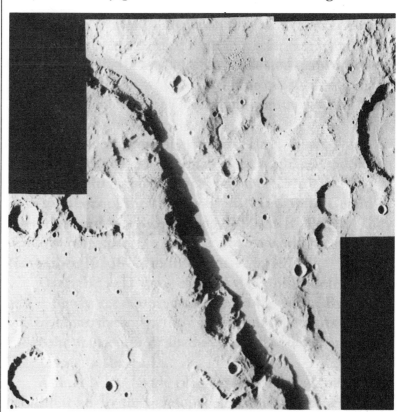

The Grand Canyon of Mars is a rift valley and the largest known canyon in the solar system, is 500 miles long, averages ten miles in width, and is about 1.3 miles deep.

cury) on November 5, 1964, destination: Mars. The mission failed. Contact was lost with the spacecraft.

Three weeks later, on November 28, NASA launched *Mariner 4*, again to voyage to Mars. On July 14, 1965, *Mariner 4* came within 6,118 miles of the surface of Mars and sent pictures back to Earth.

Every now and then in science, evidence can confuse more than clarify things. Such was the case of the first Martian photographs, which showed a bleak planet covered with craters. Mars looked very much like our own moon— a lifeless place, a dead world lacking interest. The public was disappointed.

In July and August 1969, pictures from *Mariner 6* and 7 showed more craters. It appeared more and more likely that Mars was just like the moon. Our most popular planet, it seemed, had failed us.

In November 1973, *Mariner 9* went into orbit around the red planet—the first spacecraft ever to orbit Mars. It photographed the planet over many months. Scientists were in for another Martian surprise. The first pictures showed a huge dust storm circling the whole planet. Scientists were shocked at the sheer size of this storm. For months, almost nothing could be seen of the land below through the clouds of dust.

As the air cleared and the dust settled, the photographs showed that Mars was an extraordinary place, unlike anything ever seen before. Among its remarkable features was a huge canyon, longer than the United States is wide, and 20,000 feet deep. This canyon is part of the Martian rift valley system.

There was also a high volcano, Olympus Mons. At 15 miles high, it rises about three times higher than Mount Everest. Its base measures some 345 miles (550 kilometers) in diameter—about the distance between New York City and Cleveland.

Most interesting and startling were the strange dry

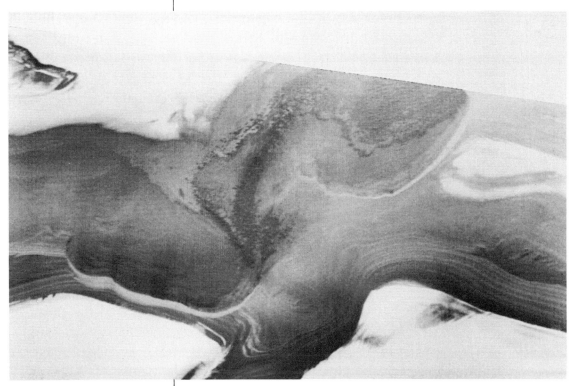

The north polar region of Mars, during a Martian summer. The picture covers an area of about 18 by 37 miles. Note the steplike formations. They are formed by ice and by layered formations of the ground beneath.

"rivers." The photographs show that they not only look like the dry rivers, or arroyos, of the American Southwest, but indicate that like them, they were formed by water. Most scientists do believe that they are the product of water erosion.

The water on Mars today is all frozen and lies mostly on the polar regions as ice caps. This ice has not melted during the time of space exploration. Instruments showed no free water on the ground or in the atmosphere as vapor. Today Mars is much drier than any desert, an exceptionally dry place. On all of Mars there may not be a single drop of liquid water.

But this is only today. In the distant past it is possible that the ice did melt and that water racing off the ice caps formed rivers lasting millions of years. Furthermore, millions of years ago, it's likely that there was a much thicker atmosphere on Mars that contained rain clouds. But in time

Mars lost its atmosphere. Its gravity is too weak to hold on to an atmosphere. Atoms of oxygen and water in the form of gas fly off into space, escaping the Martian grip of gravity.

So, it's believed that rivers once ran and canyons were gouged out. Besides the ice caps remaining today, some scientists suggest that under the ground of Mars there may be huge reservoirs of water, almost certainly frozen solid.

But what about tomorrow? Earth goes through ice ages and warmer periods, and Mars probably does, too. Someday the polar ice caps may melt. Then rivers will run again—but not as vigorously as in the past, before so much water vapor floated off into space.

The "rivers" are not the only clue to a wet past. Some of the pictures show what appear to be ancient beaches that apparently were left beside now dry lakes, even seas.

If there was once water on Mars—and the evidence shows there was for millions of years—then it is possible that life sprung up on Mars as it did on Earth. After all, life here needed water, and the same would hold true on Mars. Someplace on Mars there may be fossils that would reveal that life did exist in the distant past.

These "rivers" that *Mariner* 9 showed us rank as one of the most important space discoveries to date.

Excited and encouraged by the findings of *Mariner* 9, NASA designed and built a new type of space vehicle to meet the challenge of Mars. In July and September 1976, *Viking 1* and *Viking 2* spaceships dropped automobile-sized landers onto the surface of Mars. The landers came to rest in the middle of a bleak red desert. (The red color of the deserts and plains of Mars can be seen with one's naked eye, when Mars's orbit is at its closest to Earth. Because it is the color of blood, ancient Greeks and Romans believed that Mars was ruled by the war god, called Ares in Greece and Mars in Rome.)

Photographs taken by the landers showed windblown red sand, some rocks, and not much else. Not a living thing—not a bush or cactus or blade of grass. Above was a reddish sky; it was a strange land, a somewhat frightening place.

On board the landers were tiny weather stations. The thermometers showed that Mars is an intensely cold place. Both landers recorded the same temperatures. The coldest they registered was -80°C (-112°F) and the highest a mere -30°C (-22°F).

Some photographs revealed frost on the sand of the desert. Others showed that winds moved the sands about. Scientists concluded the color of the sky changed because of sandstorms.

Of most interest to scientists and the public were the tests for life on Mars.

Using very small but sophisticated pieces of equipment and various chemicals, the landers tested the soil around them for signs of life. Little scoopers picked up soil that was mixed with the chemicals. Equipment on board the landers analyzed the results. No positive signs of life showed up.

On the other hand, the tests do not prove that Mars lacks life. There may be life in areas far from the two locations where the landers stood. There is also a remote possibility that the tests may not have shown whatever life the landers picked up. A few scientists not satisfied with the results of the tests have expressed a minority opinion that the tests actually showed possible life forms in the soil. The majority view, however, is that no life was found by the landers. This does not necessarily mean that Mars has always lacked life. Someday in the future, Mars will be more thoroughly explored, and eventually a definite answer will be found to the nagging question of life on Mars.

Thanks to NASA's efforts and successes, we now know that Mercury, Venus, Earth, our moon, and Mars are basically similar in terms of their geology. The four giant planets, on the other hand, are very different.

JUPITER

The four giant planets—Jupiter, Saturn, Uranus, and Neptune—lie far beyond Mars. Much of the year, you can easily see Jupiter and Saturn in the night sky. Uranus is too far away to see except occasionally. Neptune, the most distant of the giant planets, can never be seen without the aid of a telescope.

Jupiter has an amazing atmosphere that is in constant motion. Storms that could shake Earth to pieces rage night and day there. Thunderstorms of unbelievable power roar all the time. Lightning bolts thousands of times larger than anything known on Earth slash the clouds.

On March 2, 1972, NASA launched *Pioneer 10*, the first spacecraft to go beyond Mars to explore the region around and very near Jupiter. *Pioneer 10* held a wide array of instruments to measure magnetism and hydrogen atoms in space, and to gather information about dust in the asteroid belt, cosmic rays, the solar wind, and other data in that distant region of the solar system. What interested most people were the close-up pictures of Jupiter.

Pioneer 11, launched April 5, 1973, came closest to Jupiter between November 18 and December 9, 1974. Unlike *Pioneer 10*, it explored a polar region of Jupiter never seen from Earth.

The two *Pioneer* spacecraft sent back exact data about the atmosphere and the chemicals in it. They showed that the planet was not a gas giant as previously thought, but was mostly a huge ocean of liquid hydrogen. Another discovery showed that millions of cubic miles of the atmosphere are at our room temperature, that is, about 68°F.

Later, two *Voyager* spacecraft went to Jupiter. Photographs taken by NASA's *Voyager 1* on March 5, 1979, and *Voyager 2* on July 9, 1979, show that the mysterious but famous red spot is really part of the atmosphere. In fact, it is a gigantic high-pressure area of cool air around which winds rage. Its red color still puzzles scientists, but it seems to be caused by traces of phosphorous chemicals. It may be made up of organic chemicals, which can form life under certain conditions. It is remotely possible that there may be life on Jupiter.

Voyager 2 discovered that Jupiter has rings around it much like those of Saturn. Jupiter's rings are much thinner than Saturn's, so we cannot see them from Earth.

Like Earth, Jupiter displays auroras (northern and southern lights) at its poles. Jupiter also has a magnetic field around it, as Earth does, but Jupiter's is far stronger. Jupiter gives off very powerful natural radio waves as well.

If you look at Jupiter through a pair of field glasses of about seven power or stronger several nights in a row, you will see the four largest moons of Jupiter. You can see them change positions after a few days. These four moons are called the Galilean satellites, because they were discovered by the great Italian scientist Galileo Galilei around 1609.

Io

During the Space Age, no moon or planet gave scientists and the public such surprises as Io, the moon closest to Jupiter.

Before the *Voyager 1* spacecraft, launched in 1977, reached the regions of space near Jupiter, all that was known about Io from photographs taken through telescopes on Earth was that it was roundish, fuzzy, and sort of orange.

Then on March 5, 1979, *Voyager* took photographs of Io from 20,000 kilometers (12,500 miles) away. The pictures arrived at the Jet Propulsion Laboratory in Pasadena, California. By March 9, 1979, astronomers, geologists, and other scientists were marveling at the strangeness of Io. Because of its color, someone said it looked like a giant pizza.

That night, after most people had left the laboratory, engineer Linda Morabito was checking out the navigational route of *Voyager 1* through space. She looked at pictures

Io, a moon of Jupiter. Its strange, highly colored surface is a result of meteorite hits and almost constant volcanic eruptions.

of Io, hoping to see key stars behind the disk of the moon that would show the location of *Voyager 1* and reveal its precise course.

Morabito could hardly believe her eyes. At the edge of Io, she saw a huge plume rising above the surface of the moon. Quickly calculating its height, she figured it rose 174 miles above the moon. She realized that a volcanic eruption might be taking place. If so, it would be the only known active volcano anywhere else but on Earth. To make sure, she spoke with many other experts. They agreed, and the information was sent on to what is called the imaging team, made up of geologists and others, who confirmed that it was indeed a volcanic eruption. On close study of the moon, they found other volcanoes were also erupting. To find an active volcano on a moon thought dead was one of the greatest surprises of the Space Age. To actually catch a volcano in the act of erupting was unbelievable luck.

Further study showed that Io's surface is covered with sulfur and sulfur dioxide. The plume was also sulfur. Io is a terribly hot, sulfurous world. The moon is heated up by the friction of Jupiter's gravity pulling and twisting it.

Of all the moons in the solar system, none is stranger, more alien than Io.

Europa

Europa, the second farthest Galilean moon from Jupiter, is entirely different from Io. Europa was photographed on July 9, 1979, by *Voyager 2* from a distance of 62,000 kilometers (38,500 miles).

Europa is almost featureless. Its surface is as smooth as a cue ball and made of ice. Underneath, however, is mostly silicate rock, like sandstone and most rocks we see on the surface of our planet.

Europa, one of the four moons of Jupiter. Most, if not all, of the surface of Europa is covered with ice about 60 miles thick. The long streaks in the ice indicate that the crust has been fractured and filled with materials from the interior.

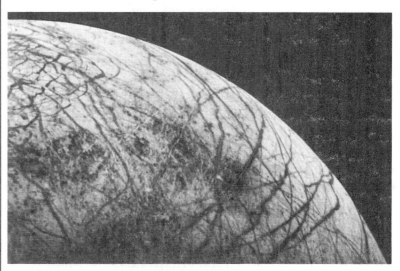

Ganymede

On March 5, 1979, *Voyager 1* took photographs of Ganymede, the third closest Galilean moon to Jupiter, from a distance of 115,000 kilometers (65,200 miles). Ganymede is a gigantic moon, larger even than the planet Mercury.

The pictures showed the ice crust of Ganymede. This ice lies on top of the huge oceans covering most, if not all, of the moon. Some continents appear darkly beneath the ice. The surface of the ice is strange and grooved with odd, irregular patterns. During the ages, occasional meteors have hit Ganymede and broken through the ice, splashing into the oceans underneath. Splashed-up white ice lies over old ice.

No moon could be more unlike our moon, which does not have a drop of water on it.

It is remotely possible that some form of life lives in the deep oceans under the ice. Someday those oceans will be explored.

Callisto

Callisto is the Galilean moon farthest from Jupiter. It was photographed by *Voyager 2* on July 8, 1979, from various distances.

In many ways, Callisto is a twin of Ganymede. It, too, is covered with a layer of ice that lies on top of an ocean. The ocean might be partly frozen, sort of slushy. The ice crust is far thicker than Ganymede's. Callisto's ice is totally covered with meteor craters. There does not seem to be a square inch that has not been hit. Because of this, scientists believe that Callisto is very old.

SATURN

Saturn, the planet with the big and dramatic rings around it, is in many ways a sister planet of Jupiter, although it is much farther away from the sun. As one would guess, Saturn is a very cold place.

On Jupiter, winds blow and storms rage because of great temperature differences in its atmosphere. Some places are extraordinarily hot and some places very cold. On Saturn, though, it is so cold that no great Jupiter-like storms can rage. Its atmosphere is much quieter and in many ways less interesting than Jupiter's.

But Saturn does have rings. For centuries these rings have puzzled astronomers, scientists, and the public. All that was known was that they were remarkably wide, and remarkably thin.

In 1979 Saturn was visited by *Pioneer 11*. But the most spectacular pictures were obtained by two *Voyager* space-

The rings of Saturn as seen from a *Voyager* spacecraft at a distance of 1.7 million miles.

craft. After photographing and exploring Jupiter and its moons, *Voyager 1* and *Voyager 2* flew on through lonely, vacant space to come to Saturn, which is almost a billion miles from the sun.

In 1980 and 1981, *Voyager 1* and *Voyager 2* began to photograph the rings of Saturn, which are a few miles wide at their widest. From analysis of the pictures, it appears the rings are made up of small particles, mostly "snowballs" and rocks. Moons circling around Saturn "shepherd" the rings, which means that the pull of their gravity keeps the rings from becoming either wider or narrower. In places some rings look as though they are braided. No one knows why. In spite of close views and spectacular photographs of the rings, they remain quite mysterious.

The two *Voyager* spacecraft also photographed a number of Saturn's many moons. All except the huge moon Titan were shown to be lifeless worlds covered with rock or ice. Titan, however, was different; there is a remote chance that life could exist on it.

Titan

If explorers were to look for life someplace other than Earth, where would they go? Mars comes to mind; so does the atmosphere of Jupiter, and possibly the ocean on Jupiter's moon Ganymede. But first one might go to Saturn's moon Titan.

With a diameter of 2,575 miles, Titan is slightly smaller than Jupiter's Ganymede, which has a diameter of 2,640 miles. (Earth's moon is 2,160 miles.) Ganymede is the largest moon in the solar system, Titan the second, and Neptune's Triton the third largest. All three are larger than the planet Mercury.

What is so amazing about Titan is that it has an atmosphere. (An atmosphere is the covering of gases that surrounds a moon or planet.) No other moon, as far as we

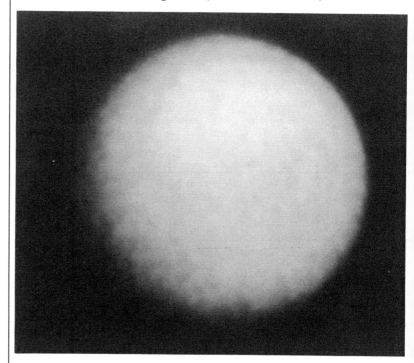

Titan, the largest of Saturn's moons, is one of the few moons in the solar system known to have an atmosphere. The atmosphere surrounding Titan probably contains hydrocarbons, from which life may have arisen. There is a remote possibility that some form of life exists on Titan.

know, has a true atmosphere. Titan's atmosphere is ten times thicker than ours on Earth—that is, there is ten times more gas per square foot on Titan.

The atmosphere of Titan is made up mostly of nitrogen (so is ours), argon, methane, and hydrogen. It also has much smaller quantities of several other gases, ten of which are organic chemicals, the kind that can form life.

On November 12, 1980, *Voyager 1* tested the atmosphere of Titan and found that it has many more chemicals than ours. It is a rich atmosphere—and a strange one, for it lacks oxygen or water vapor.

Various organic compounds form in this atmosphere and drop to the surface of Titan. The whole moon is probably covered with oozy substances which might be similar to crude oil. If the organic chemicals in those substances formed some type of life, it would be life very different from any we know, due to the lack of water.

The sky on Titan has clouds of methane gas. Sometimes a liquid methane "rain" falls. There are probably methane oceans, or natural gas oceans, on Titan.

In spite of its rains, oceans, and possible life forms, Titan is not a tropical place. Exactly the opposite—it is terribly cold. The temperature measured by *Voyager 1* was -319°F.

Since we have no idea what the surface of Titan really looks like because it is obscured by high clouds, NASA plans someday to obtain a map of Titan with the help of a spacecraft carrying radar equipment. Probes will then be dropped onto the hard parts of the surface. Eventually, decades in the future, astronauts may go to Titan to collect and bring back the organic chemicals and whatever life they might find there.

By knowing how life formed on Titan—if it did—we will have a much better idea of how life formed on planet Earth. And there are billions of stars—more stars in the universe than grains of sand on all the beaches of Earth.

If Titan has life, then it stands to reason that so would countless moons and planets that circle the billions upon billions of stars.

URANUS

On March 13, 1781, the astronomer Sir William Herschel realized that Uranus was a planet and not just another dim star.

Uranus is green, not because of vegetation, but because of chemical actions in its cold atmosphere. Like Saturn, Uranus has rings, but nothing as dramatic as the other planet's.

Uranus is 1.8 billion miles from the sun—seventeen times as far from the sun as Earth. The sun's warmth on Uranus is 1/290th what it is on Earth. It is a cold, lonely place.

In January 1986, *Voyager 2* passed by Uranus, photographed it, and recorded its temperature and magnetic field. Its temperature was -346°F. Oddly enough, *Voyager 2* revealed, Uranus lies on its side. Every 42 years, its poles are aimed almost at the sun. The planet circles the sun every 84 years. In spite of the fact that one pole—the one toward the sun—should be much warmer than the other pole, this was not so. The temperature of the planet was quite even.

Pictures of the planet show some wispy clouds. Over the poles lie what appears to be smog of natural hydrocarbons. Otherwise the planet completely lacks details; it looks like a beautiful blue-green ball in space.

However, despite *Voyager 2*'s trip, not much is known about this remote planet.

Miranda

Uranus and its moons are the most distant bodies *Voyager 2* photographed. Miranda is a small Uranian moon mostly covered with ice. *Voyager 2* pictures of Miranda show strange patterns on its surface. For one thing, a large trapezoid area shows never-before-seen chevron zigzags in it. Parts of the moon are white, because of the ice, but other parts are almost black because of rocks. Scientists at the Jet Propulsion Laboratory at first could not figure this out.

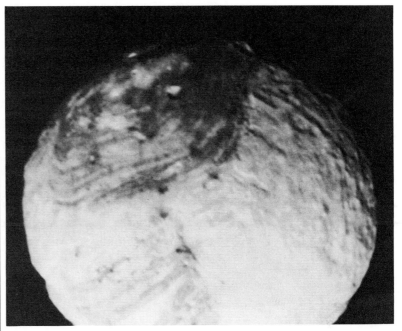

Miranda, the smallest of five moons of the planet Uranus, photographed by *Voyager 2* on January 24, 1986, from a distance of 91,000 miles. Note the parallel lines. They are fault lines where the moon broke and came together again due to the impact of meteorites. Many craters can also be seen.

After intensive study, they came to the conclusion that Miranda had been hit by large comets and meteoroids, which had actually torn the moon apart. Fragments of Miranda rushed off into space after being hit. But the force of gravity pulled pieces of the moon back together again, forming a new moon. This happened many times, so that Miranda has been completely reformed over and over again from fragments. The photographs showed a moon rather recently formed, geologically speaking, from fragments. The trapezoid area is a huge block of solid material. The chevrons show where it is settling. As it settles, ripple marks form the chevrons.

In addition to the chevrons, the photographs showed remarkable ice cliffs, which rise ten miles high and are the tallest, sheerest cliffs yet seen in the solar system. Enormous canyons that would dwarf the Grand Canyon of Arizona are also visible.

This singular world shows us how space exploration turns up strange and exotic things as it continues, even billions of miles away.

NEPTUNE AND PLUTO

No spacecraft has flown to Neptune yet, but *Voyager 2* is headed in its direction and should fly by and photograph it sometime in 1989 or 1990. NASA has no spacecraft going to Pluto, the most distant planet in our solar system.

BEYOND THE SOLAR SYSTEM

NASA has no plans at this time to explore the world beyond the solar system, not even the nearest stars. They are much too distant.

Even so, some spacecraft launched by NASA will leave the solar system.

Pioneer 10 was launched on March 3, 1972. It passed by Jupiter on December 3, 1973, and took photographs of it. By now it has left the solar system. *Pioneer 10* carries a plaque showing a picture of a man and woman and information about Earth and its location. The man holds up his hand in greeting. Greeting to whom? To whatever intelligent being picks up the plaque light-years away from our solar system and thousands, perhaps millions of years from now.

After *Voyager 2* passes Neptune, it will head out of the solar system to reach interstellar space sometime in the early days of the twenty-first century. On it are recordings of Earth sounds—songs from various nations, bird songs,

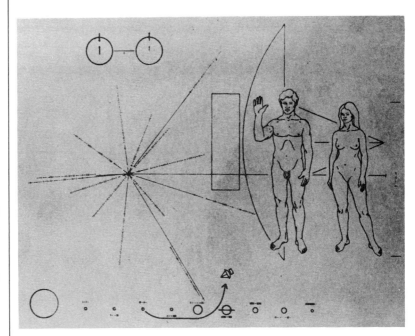

Millions of years from now, intelligent beings on some far-away planet may find this plaque in the *Pioneer F* spacecraft, now headed toward the distant stars. It shows a man and woman standing next to the *Pioneer F.* The lines and symbols indicate when and where *Pioneer* was launched. The lower images show the solar system and the route of *Pioneer F* from the earth—the third planet from the sun.

and whale songs. It also carries photographs of scenes on Earth.

Although NASA will never hear from *Pioneer 10* or *Voyager 2* once they reach the greatest void of all, at least it has sent its greetings onward. We are trying to make contact with our distant neighbors, if any exist.

So far, our exploration of the solar system reveals no other life in the universe, but the plants and animals of our home—Earth. We appear to be alone, but it is natural for us to wonder. . .

10

The Earth in Space

When we think of NASA, we usually think of the race to the moon or spacecraft going to other planets. But NASA has been engaged in other important activities focused on our own planet. Thanks to NASA's many efforts, we know a great deal more about our planet than we did a mere thirty years ago.

It is difficult for young people today to realize how much of our knowledge about planet Earth we owe to the Space Age. It is hard to believe, for example, that until the end of World War II some balloons had risen only 100,000 feet above the ground—hardly 20 miles. Though the view awed people then, we now know how little the view up there showed. Some cloud patterns could be seen, and the curvature of the earth could just barely be made out.

After World War II, American scientists working with Wernher von Braun attached some cameras to captured German *V2* rockets and sent them over 100 miles high. Pictures showed more of the earth below—mainly areas near White Sands, New Mexico.

In the early 1960s photographs taken by orbiting astronauts began to reveal a world we had never seen before. Among the many photographs were clear views of large sections of North Africa. Many previously unknown geologic features were revealed. We could see how much of North Africa was desert, how much croplands. Areas unknown to European explorers, and perhaps not even to Arab explorers, showed up. Other photographs revealed much that was unknown about the Himalayas. Extinct volcanoes less than a hundred miles from America's southern border were discovered in Mexico. For the first time ever, we could look straight down on a huge tropical storm. Ocean currents not seen from ships or even airplanes showed up in the photographs.

Obviously, space gave us new ways of seeing our own planet.

OUR WEATHER

Of all the photographs made from space since the early 1960s, the most valuable are those that show large weather systems in action.

As soon as the Space Age began, NASA sent weather satellites into orbit. The earliest of them, the TIROS (Television and Infra-Red Observation Satellites), were first launched April 1, 1960. They carried two television cameras aimed at the earth. The images they sent back were made into black-and-white stills. Between 1960 and 1965, over 500,000 pictures of weather systems in all parts of the earth were obtained from TIROS satellites.

Meteorologists were surprised to see that far more of the planet has cloud cover than they had imagined. The birth, growth, and death of hurricanes and other storms were easily studied in detail, as was the interaction between cold and warm air masses. TIROS almost immediately gave meteorologists a new and far better understanding of the

A weather satellite. This Geosynchronous Operational Environmental Satellite B (GOES-B) is designed to gather atmospheric information for the National Oceanic and Atmospheric Administration.

earth's weather. Daily forecasts became more accurate. The pictures aided long-term forecasts as well.

Also on board TIROS weather satellites were infrared sensors that recorded the temperature of the earth's surface and cloud cover.

The TIROS satellites were followed by ESSA (Environmental Science Services Administration) satellites. They were much like TIROS satellites.

Nimbus weather satellites were considerably more sophisticated. They scanned the earth in all wavelengths from ultraviolet to infrared. Nimbus satellites could record temperature readings at various depths of the atmosphere and obtain humidity readings. The pictures Nimbus satellites obtained, in various wavelengths, proved extremely valuable to many others besides meteorologists. They could show where there was pack ice, for instance. Commercial shippers, fishermen, and others could determine where ice-free channels lay, or take educated guesses about when bays and channels would be free of ice. This saved ship captains time and money, for they knew when and when not to sail into northern harbors. Nimbus pictures could also show the difference between cold and warm ocean currents. Shifts in the Gulf Stream and other currents could easily be detected. Since fish follow certain currents and not others, such information was valuable to fishermen.

Greece, as photographed from ERTS-1 spacecraft at an altitude of 569 miles. Note the clear details. Athens is in the extreme upper right. This and other photographs like it help experts gather valuable information about crops, geology, the environment, and weather conditions.

Nimbus could show snow cover, helping people predict spring runoffs. Since western farmers and ranchers depend on the spring runoffs for most of their yearly water supplies, such information is of extreme value to them.

The benefits derived by weather forecasters and others from Nimbus are endless. Before satellites were used, the nations of the world spent tens, even hundreds of millions of dollars a year gathering information about the weather. The satellites do a far better job more swiftly and at only a fraction of the cost.

THE EARTH'S ATMOSPHERE

We live at the bottom of a sea of air called the atmosphere. The top of the atmosphere is roughly 300 miles above us. It is difficult to say just where it ends, for it gets thinner and thinner at the top.

NASA satellites have studied the atmosphere in great detail. Even so, a great deal remains to be known about it.

Meteorologists and oceanographers are deeply interested in how the atmosphere and oceans of the world interact. They want to know, for example, just how the oceans pick up heat from the atmosphere, and why the atmosphere and oceans cool down at times. They want to know how various energy rays from the sun influence the atmosphere.

All the time, Earth's atmosphere is bombarded by electrical particles from the sun, gamma rays, ultraviolet rays, visible light rays, infrared rays, natural-occurring radio waves, and powerful cosmic rays from deep space. Much needs to be known about how all these change our atmosphere.

At the same time, gases from industries rise into the atmosphere. Carbon dioxide is one such gas. Burning forests release it, as do all fires. Scientists believe that increasing amounts of carbon dioxide are slowly warming up

The top of hurricane Elana, photographed from a *Discovery* satellite on September 2, 1985. The eye of the hurricane is the dark hole in the clouds. The storm clouds, driven by high winds, move around the eye. Such pictures from space allow meteorologists to see a hurricane, track its movement, and warn people about its approach.

the atmosphere of Earth. If so, polar ice will melt, and the sea levels around the world will rise higher and higher. Unpredictable changes will take place in the climate. These changes are being watched by NASA satellites. As we will see later, NASA will take part in the international "Geosphere-Biosphere Program" to study the atmosphere.

NASA satellites as well as high-altitude rockets monitor many changes in the atmosphere. They detect changes in solar energy coming to the earth, chemical changes in the upper atmosphere, and pollution.

High-altitude rockets can pick up actual air samples, from sea level to the edge of space itself.

By photographing the greening of the hemispheres during each of their springtimes, satellites can show rapid or slow earth warm-ups, which indicate future weather patterns. Pictures of cloud covers show whether this planet is cooling down in places. Since bare earth, and especially earth covered with snow and seas covered with ice, reflects heat away from our planet, satellites can determine heat loss this way as well.

The best way of keeping track of the complexities of the atmosphere is through satellites and high-altitude rockets of NASA and other countries.

MAPS AND MORE MAPS

Today hundreds of thousands of photographs have been taken of the earth from space. These are not, of course, just photographs. Each one is also a map—and a very accurate map—of either the whole planet or some feature of it as seen from space. This feature might be a city and its streets. (Some photographs, which are military secrets, are said to show the license plates of Russian automobiles.)

The space photographs are used for hundreds of different purposes. They provide, for instance, a look at world

A view of the east coast of North America from the weather satellite SMS-1. The SMS-1 can take pictures of the clouds covering the earth both day and night and thus keep a constant watch on the earth's rapidly changing weather systems.

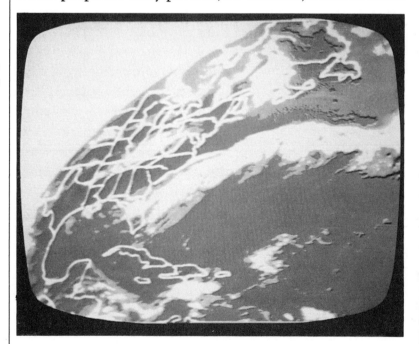

crops. Experts can tell how the major crops of the world, such as rice, wheat, and corn, are doing. They can see how healthy crops are and when they might be harvested, and thus predict what farm prices might be. Forest reserves, expanding desert areas, and crop damage can be studied. Future timber prices and falling land prices can be calculated.

Maps obtained from satellites are also useful to engineers planning new locations for new highways, dams, and wharves. City planners use them in determining where new suburbs should be located. Amazingly, the maps obtained from satellites have located locust swarms in Africa and helped people control these insects. There is, in fact, no end to their uses.

MINERALS AND OIL

Each year, the world uses huge quantities of iron, copper, tin, aluminum, and other metals, as well as fuels such as coal and oil. All these valuable resources are found in the rocks or soils of the earth.

Geologists need to know where to look for new earth resources. They can search on the ground, but exploration costs are extraordinarily high. Even so, billions of dollars are spent annually, worldwide, on new explorations. Satellites can help geologists. NASA has sent up several important satellites designed especially for the exploration of valuable minerals and fuels. Among them were two identical *Landsats*, launched in a circumpolar orbit, which covered the whole surface of the earth.

Landsats carried sophisticated sensor systems. There was a scanner that gathered information about the earth using four different wavelengths. Three separate television cameras, each using different wavelengths, could view a section of the earth at once. By combining the colors of the wavelengths, brilliantly colored and easy-to-use "false" color pictures of the earth's geological structures could be obtained. Scientists can see many details of the surface that would otherwise be missed. *Landsats* changed geologists' methods of prospecting for resources.

Landsat false color images make it easier for economic geologists seeking new resources to see stress points on the earth's surface, such as earthquake faults, where oil deposits sometimes get trapped; stained soil where copper, iron, and titanium might be found; geologic features difficult to recognize on the ground, such as domes, which often indicate oil resources; and layers of underlying rocks where valuable resources such as coal, oil, and gas are usually found.

Through the use of *Landsat* false color images, geologists and others can see the world more clearly and in far greater detail.

COMMUNICATIONS VIA COMMUNICATION SATELLITES

Before the Space Age, it was possible to send shortwave radio waves upward from the earth. High above us, about 30 to 300 miles, they bounced off a layer of ionized particles in the ionosphere. Such radio waves could be received thousands of miles away. But there was a catch. The ionosphere often changes its nature, and can be disturbed by solar radiation. At times radio waves fail and communications are lost. In short, communications over hundreds and thousands of miles can be risky and unreliable. One could, at times, send radio broadcasts over long distances by shortwave radio. All other forms of radio signals could be sent only locally. TV signals were the most difficult to send. They could only be sent from one station to another if, and only if, they were sent through cables or the stations were within sight of one another.

With the Space Age, all that changed. A communications revolution took place—and is still going on today.

As early as December 1958, radio messages were sent to Earth from a tape recorder inside a U.S. *Atlas* rocket that orbited the planet. It broadcast a Christmas message by President Eisenhower.

In 1960, a 52-inch sphere orbited the earth. This communications satellite was called SCORE (Signal Communication by Orbiting Relay Equipment). With power from photoelectric cells that drew energy from the sunlight, it relayed teletype, voice, and facsimile data, which, for example, is used to send graphics to newspapers in distant cities, between ground stations. This was possible because radio waves in some wavelengths can go through the ionosphere, reach such an orbiting satellite, and be returned to another place on Earth.

At the same time, NASA bounced radio signals off the 100-foot-diameter *Echo 1* satellite and the 135-foot-diameter *Echo 2* satellite.

A real breakthrough in worldwide communications came when the American Telephone and Telegraph Company built *Telstar*. The *Telstar* satellite was a 32-inch sphere covered with solar cells. Messages from one ground-based station could be sent to it and retransmitted by *Telstar* to another ground station hundreds, even thousands of miles away. Unfortunately, *Telstar 1* was damaged by radiation in the Van Allen belt. But before it failed, it proved that it could carry 600 telephone circuits at once.

In 1964, Intelsat—the International Telecommunications Satellite Consortium—was set up by a number of nations to produce and operate international communications. Some of the satellites belonging to Intelsat can carry as many as 9,000 telephone circuits.

Right now there are dozens of different types of communications satellites orbiting the earth. All developed countries have several up, and so have many third world countries such as India.

The breakthrough in communications that NASA's satellites fostered is a prime example of the value of a space program. It is many times less expensive to send telephone conversations, television programs, radio broadcasts, and the like by way of these satellites than by ground cables or relay stations. Countless hundreds of millions of dollars have been saved. Moreover, the satellites are far more reliable and much faster.

Not only that, they have brought countries closer together. People all over the world can watch a coronation, see a favorite soccer match, or receive coverage of a major news story as it happens. Beyond the economic benefits, there are numerous social benefits. Many telecommunications can, for example, send educational programs to small villages in poor areas all over the world.

As in the past, future efforts will continue to make communications satellites better and better.

11

Skylab

People will someday remember that Skylab was the first space station.

Oddly enough, NASA did not originally plan to build a space station. But scientists and NASA officials realized that they could convert an empty *Saturn* rocket into housing, connect an *Apollo* module and other equipment to it, and create a reasonably large space station. The more this plan was considered, the better it looked. A space station was not only possible to build, but also inexpensive. Moreover, NASA saw great advantages in having a space station up. Many experiments could be performed in it, and the long-term effects of space travel could be studied when astronauts lived in the space station for weeks on end. So NASA went ahead with the plan and called this space station Skylab.

Skylab was sent into space on May 14, 1973. It was nearly a disaster: The drag of the atmosphere almost tore off the meteoroid shield over the laboratory; a large solar panel came loose and disappeared into space; another became entangled; and temperatures inside the spacecraft soared to 300°F.

Skylab as seen from the command and service module, which later docked with Skylab, making it much larger and longer. Skylab served as the world's first space station. Note the solar panels on the right.

The crew that arrived in space eleven days later was able to do something about the situation. They set up a covering that looked like a parasol over the roasting spacecraft. Eventually the temperatures inside fell, and the crew was able to dock and go inside the laboratory.

Though it was not nearly as large as future space stations will be, Skylab was, nevertheless, the largest spacecraft ever to be in space. The orbiting Skylab weighed 100 tons. It was 118 feet long and 22 feet in diameter at its widest (far larger than most city apartments).

There were four stories in Skylab. On the first story were a workshop, a shower, a lavatory, and a kitchen. The astronauts slept here as well.

The second story contained the big storage areas for water tanks, film, and frozen foods. It was used primarily as a workshop.

The third story contained the controls for the solar telescope, which was used for the constant study of the sun, and a laboratory for the processing of materials. Earth observations were made from here.

The fourth story was the *Apollo* command module, which had brought the astronauts up to Skylab and would take them home again. While the astronauts were in space, they did not use the command module.

The first crew entered Skylab May 25, 1973, and stayed in it for 28 days. The crew members were Charles Conrad, Dr. Joseph Kerwin, and Paul J. Weitz.

Like the two crews that would follow, they had their work cut out for them. First they had to assess the damage caused by the heat. Many chemicals in the space laboratory, medical supplies, and photographic supplies were destroyed.

The most important Skylab experiment was to see how humans could adapt and fare during a long stay in space. The astronauts in Skylab enjoyed more room than had any other astronauts. They could wander about inside the large spacecraft, floating weightlessly from place to place. To keep in good physical shape, they all did exercises for 30 minutes a day. There were bicycle machines and other equipment aboard so that they could work out and keep up their strength.

The second most important experiment was the astronauts' survey of the sun with their telescope and on-board solar observatory. For the first time, small changes in the sun, never before seen from Earth, could be carefully observed. A vast amount of information about the sun and its behavior was gained. The sun is a very active star. At all times its hot gases rise, burn, change, and descend back into it. Huge storms rage. Flames much larger than the earth rise from its surface.

The astronauts also turned their telescope toward the distant stars. They watched and photographed them so that

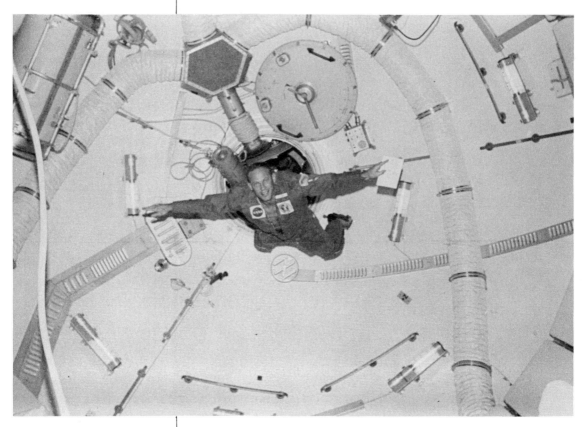

they could see their infrared and ultraviolet rays. They obtained new and different views of the stars and especially of dust clouds near them.

The astronauts also kept a close watch on several experiments set up by U.S. high school students. One involved a common cross spider, which they named Arabella. They wanted to see how Arabella would weave her web in a weightless environment. Here on Earth, spiders weave their webs by hanging from them. Without gravity to pull her down, how would she do it? Her first web was an absolute mess. But after a while, Arabella adjusted to her weightless condition and wove webs almost as good as the webs she normally wove on Earth.

Another experiment involved some mummichog minnows. How would fish adapt to weightlessness, and how would fish eggs hatch? The minnows quickly adapted to weightlessness and their eggs hatched normally. The baby minnows seemed already adapted to weightlessness.

These experiments showed that at least some animals could readily adapt to the weightless conditions of space travel.

When the first Skylab crew returned to Earth, they were tested extensively to see the effects of their long stay. The tests showed that human beings could fare very well in space. For unknown reasons, there were problems with a loss of calcium in the bones, and the weightless environment caused some nausea and minor problems with a weakening of their hearts and legs, from which the astronauts quickly recovered upon their return. Otherwise, the astronauts were in excellent shape. In fact, they improved in one unexpected way. While in space they required less sleep and were more active than they would have been on Earth.

After the first crew left, Skylab floated empty through the sky high above the earth for a little over a month. Then a new crew entered it. They would continue with all the experiments.

The new crew members were Alan L. Bean, Owen K. Garriott, and Jack R. Lousma. They would stay in Skylab for 59 days, from July 28 to September 25, 1973.

Members of the third and final crew were Gerald P. Carr, Edward G. Gibson, and William R. Pogue. They would stay in space for 84 days, then a world record, from November 16, 1973, until February 8, 1974.

Over the next few years, Skylab's orbit deteriorated and it slowly got closer and closer to the earth. By 1979 it was touching the top of the earth's atmosphere. As it began to hit the molecules of air they slowed it down and it fell ever closer to the earth.

At first NASA made plans to boost Skylab into higher orbit, but finally they announced that it would be allowed to fall to Earth. No one knew where it might land. The idea that it might crash anyplace, of course, made people nervous. Since its orbit took it mostly over oceans, however, it was unlikely to hit land.

Finally, on July 11, 1979, at 12:30 A.M. on its 34,981st orbit, Skylab plowed into the earth's atmosphere and broke up, fiery parts of it falling toward Earth. Most parts crashed into the ocean, but some pieces landed on the Australian desert near Kalgoorlie and Esperance. A few people saw the flaming debris fall. Fewer still felt their houses and ground shake. There were no injuries. In fact, it took days for anyone to find the fragments.

Skylab is gone, but not its many lessons. It showed some remarkable things. For example, Skylab, though a superior piece of high-technology equipment, could not last as an unmanned spacecraft. The problems that arose with it were all solved by human beings. It showed how men and machines can work together to accomplish complicated missions.

Skylab revealed important medical lessons as well. The astronauts who worked on it for weeks at a time went downhill physically during the first 30 to 40 days. For example, the number of red blood cells fell off. But oddly, after the fortieth day, the health and well-being of the astronauts improved. Scientists and doctors here and in the Soviet Union are trying to find out why.

Another finding was that astronauts separated from families, friends, and day-to-day activities on Earth did not seem to suffer emotionally in space. (It might be added that some Russian astronauts who have been in space for longer periods of time have suffered emotional problems: mild depression, quick tempers, and other symptoms.) The astronauts proved, too, that human beings in space could plan, create, and carry out original experiments.

The fact that nothing dramatic occurred, that the astronauts in Skylab acted normally, was in essence the drama

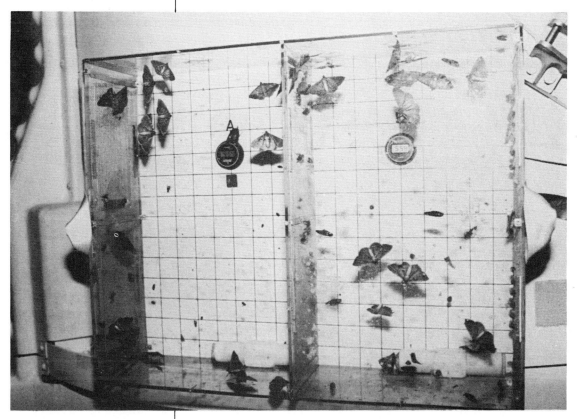

These moths, bees, and flies went into space for an eight-day trip in March 1982. They were part of an experiment designed by 18-year-old Todd Nelson, who won a nationwide contest for the best space experiments devised by schoolchildren. Nelson tested how insects would fly in weightless conditions and respond to a spaceflight. The results showed the moths to be the most active insects during the test.

of the trip. Skylab proved that humans in space can be human.

So the first space station was a success. NASA had challenged the unknown with it and had benefited in many unexpected ways. With Skylab, the door to America's future space stations has been opened.

12

The Space Shuttle

Up until the late 1960s, NASA had devoted almost all of its attention to the moon race. As a moon landing loomed ever closer, many scientists and engineers in NASA and in American industry began to wonder what to do next in space.

There was, of course, a universe with no known limits to aim for. New and better satellites were needed for communications, for weather reports, and so on. Some suggested moon colonies. Many NASA officials, politicians, and especially the public wanted to see a manned exploration of Mars. Others proposed a space station, much larger than Skylab, that would be like a large combined hotel, office, factory, and laboratory orbiting our planet.

Looking over these and many other ideas, NASA began to see that a space station would be most useful. It could serve as a stepping-stone for the exploration of space; it would be the key to many future programs. Only with the help of a space station, for instance, could a manned trip to Mars be undertaken. A space station could serve as an intermediate place for the large rockets needed for a trip to Mars to be made or loaded with fuel. It would also be necessary for establishing a moon colony. And inside a space station could be factories for manufacturing chemicals, metals, medicines, and other products that can be made only in weightless conditions.

In short, a space station was needed sooner or later, and the sooner the better. The next question became how to build one in Earth orbit over a hundred miles above the surface of the earth.

Two ways were proposed. One called for a rocket to carry astronauts up into orbit in a module. Once the module was in orbit, the rocket would fall back to Earth, never to be used again. While in orbit, astronauts could leave their module on "space walks" to build the space station piece by piece. After their work was done, the astronauts could get back into their space module and return to Earth.

This plan had a great disadvantage. On each trip, a rocket costing millions of dollars would be wasted.

The second way called for a space shuttle, which could leave Earth and go into orbit. Once in orbit, its large primary rocket could parachute to Earth. Astronauts could leave the space shuttle and work on the space station. After finishing their work, they would ride the space shuttle back to Earth. The space shuttle could return to orbit within a few days or weeks to do more work. In addition, the large space shuttle could easily carry aloft American and foreign satellites, science laboratories, and other large loads.

The space shuttle method appealed to officials, scientists, and engineers at NASA. They began brainstorming and drawing up various plans. The one they liked best called for a "space ferry" that would go into orbit and then glide back to Earth. Rockets would lift it into space, fall away, and later be recovered at sea. The ferry would continue its journey into space and go into orbit. While circling the earth, it could use small rockets to change from one orbit to another. In this way it could move about in space quite easily. But it would need to glide, without power, back to Earth.

It was a daring plan, and it raised many questions. After intensive study, a design was finally drawn up and costs figured out. Then NASA submitted plans for the space shuttle to President Nixon.

PRESIDENT RICHARD M. NIXON AND THE SPACE SHUTTLE

During Nixon's time in office (1969 to 1974), NASA went through major changes as it made the complicated transition from the moon race to the space shuttle program. Before the agency could go forward with the space shuttle, NASA needed both congressional and presidential backing.

High NASA officials approached Nixon to inform him of the shuttle plans and seek his support. This request presented Nixon with difficulties. He knew that with the moon landings a success, the American public and Congress would consider a space shuttle as an anticlimax. Though it appeared to be necessary to future space efforts, it lacked all the drama and excitement of the moon race. A canny politician, Nixon knew that to present Congress and the American public with a proposal for a space shuttle was not likely to inspire the same enthusiasm and support that Kennedy had received in making his astounding challenge to the nation.

Nixon also knew that although a large portion of the public and the majority of congressmen favored a continuation of space programs, they wanted them to move forward at a more moderate pace. Few in the public and fewer in Congress were willing to continue giving NASA the huge funding it had received in the 1960s at the rate of $4 billion a year. Nixon was on the spot.

As NASA officials described the pros and cons of the

space shuttle mostly in terms of costs, Nixon, who was a space fan to begin with, became convinced that a space shuttle would be the key to America's future in space. He okayed the preliminary plans and promised to approach Congress, which he did January 5, 1972.

The space shuttle met with strong opposition in Congress. Senator Walter Mondale, a major critic, called it a worse folly than the SST (the supersonic transport, which Congress had earlier turned down) and cited its enormous costs. While he favored space exploration, he felt the expense of the space shuttle would end up far greater than the $5.5–6.5 billion figure NASA was claiming, and that the money would be better used to solve problems on Earth.

Senator William Proxmire also spoke out against the space shuttle, calling it "an outrageous distortion of budgetary priorities. . . . The president has chosen the space shuttle over money for schools, for health, housing, mass transit, environmental needs, and other vital programs."

Proxmire's remarks hit a nerve. Many in the public agreed with him and strongly preferred monies to be spent in the ways he spelled out. Several in Congress called the space shuttle a "senseless extravaganza in space."

Naturally there were voices raised in favor of the shuttle. Senator Edward Gurney commented, "It is extremely important to the United States to have a continuing and viable space program, because technology is the strength of any great industrial nation," and many agreed.

After all sides were heard from, pro and con, Congress approved the funding.

Yet the importance of the space shuttle program cannot be stressed too much. It would be the centerpiece of NASA's efforts from 1970 until now and would shape the future of NASA for years to come. As we know today, the space shuttle would be controversial—it would cost too much, prove difficult to build, run way over budget, leave less money for other vital science programs in NASA, fall forever behind schedule, always need more repairs than originally planned, and worst of all, cause the deaths of seven men and women in January 1986.

No major effort by NASA to date has been so open to criticism, so controversial as the space shuttle. This does not suggest that it was either a mistake or a wise choice. There is no way of knowing yet whether the technological and scientific advances of the space shuttle will, in the end, justify the enormous economic and human expense.

The space shuttle program, in any event, became a reality.

BUILDING THE SPACE SHUTTLE

The space shuttle is the most complicated form of transportation ever designed, manufactured, and tested. Even after Nixon's approval, many changes were made in its design. By June 1975, 34,000 people were working on the shuttle. Even then, NASA was faced with one problem after another.

Because the shuttle had to be reusable, its surfaces could not burn up on reentry into the earth's atmosphere as had the surfaces of *Mercury, Gemini,* and *Apollo* capsules. Among the many problems, the most important and most difficult to deal with were the heat tiles. They were to be placed on parts of the space shuttle that would heat up most as it reentered the earth's atmosphere. The heat was enough to melt metals; only ceramic tiles could withstand such temperatures. They proved to be incredibly difficult to make and to place securely on the space shuttle. Even today this problem has not been solved with complete satisfaction. To test how secure the ceramic tiles were, the entire space shuttle had to be lifted high up into the air and shaken inside a huge building to see if it could withstand the vibrations of lift-off.

NASA also had to find out if it was possible for booster rockets to be recovered from space. The booster rockets had to lift the space shuttle into space and then drop toward the earth, their descent slowed by parachutes that could land them gently in the ocean.

The wings presented a particular problem. Not only did they have to withstand the tremendous strains of reentry, which could well burn them away or break them off, but they also had to be able to be used as glider wings.

In addition to everything else, a 747 airplane had to be rebuilt to transport the space shuttle from California to Florida, and to carry it piggyback into the air for a test flight.

Finally, to the cheers of thousands, in August 1977 a specially designed 747 carried the space shuttle high above a California desert. The airplane took a steep dive, releasing the space shuttle to lift and glide away into the air. The pilots in the space shuttle took it to a smooth landing.

One might think that after such a successful test flight, the space shuttle would be sent up to orbit the earth. But almost four more years of hard work went into the space shuttle program before the first launching.

SPACE SHUTTLE *COLUMBIA* IN ORBIT

On April 12, 1981, the space shuttle *Columbia* lifted-off from Cape Canaveral. It was one of the strangest sights ever seen in the history of the space program. The space shuttle seemed so tiny next to the huge central rocket to which it was attached. This rocket carried liquid oxygen and liquid hydrogen. Attached to the main central rocket were two booster rockets packed with solid fuel. Later they would drop off and be recovered and used again.

At lift-off, the rocket engines spewed out a huge cloud of flame, and the space shuttle moved upward. As planned, rockets were released to drop. Above the Florida skies, the

Astronaut John Young, commander of the first space shuttle, *Orbiter*, in the cabin of the *Columbia*. With him is astronaut Robert Crippen, the pilot.

space shuttle rolled over and continued into space by itself. While in orbit, it performed beautifully, controlled by commander John Young and pilot Robert Crippen.

Then came the worrisome part. Could a pilot take the giant "glider," which lacked any engines whatsoever, to a safe landing?

Two days later, after orbiting the earth, the *Columbia* entered the earth's atmosphere. Despite all precautions, some tiles fell off, but no damage occurred. The great spacecraft circled high above the California desert, and then the pilot came in for a perfect landing at Edwards Air Force Base. A new era in space had begun.

Though the *Columbia* worked exceptionally well, more problems arose that required more work to be done on the shuttle. Months passed before the next space shuttle went into orbit. It, too, worked very well in space. After four successful test flights, NASA declared the space shuttle fully operational.

Between flights, however, expensive and time-consuming repairs had to be made. It always took months to prepare the space shuttles for their flights.

Critics complained that the whole point of the space shuttle was that it could be used over and over again on a regular basis. It had been designed to go into orbit many times a year. But space shuttle flights rarely met schedules and were too few and far between. The truth was that the space shuttle constantly required additional funds. Billions of dollars more than the estimated budget went into the space shuttle program.

Others pointed out the many successes of the space shuttle. Because the space shuttle could be fully equipped with scientific instruments—even a space laboratory—astronauts could carry out many useful experiments. Its huge cargo bay was used to carry satellites into space and release them into orbit, as well as to pick up damaged satellites and bring them back to Earth for repairs. And the cargo bay promised to offset some of the expenses of the shuttle: NASA proposed that research groups, academic institutions, private industry, individuals, and foreign countries could rent space in the cargo bay for a fee to carry out approved experiments.

The space shuttle *Columbia* lands at Edwards Air Force Base in California after a mission of ten days, seven hours, 47 minutes, and 23 seconds.

A NEW KIND OF ASTRONAUT

If controversy continued to surround the expense of the space shuttle program, near-universal support for NASA astronauts continued as before.

With the space shuttle came a new era in the recruitment and training of astronauts. Advances in computerization and in launching equipment and procedures changed the requirements for astronauts. No longer were experienced test pilots who could withstand grueling physical trials the only ones allowed to go into space. Flying in a spacecraft had become for all but the pilots almost entirely computerized. Technical advances had greatly reduced the physical stresses—especially the G forces—encountered in space travel. With only one pilot really necessary to run the craft, the remainder of the astronauts could be specialists in many other fields—physics, chemistry, geology, and so on.

So it was that the first American woman in space was not a test pilot but a physicist.

Sally Ride, The First American Woman in Space

On June 18, 1983, the first American woman went into space to orbit the earth. (Two Soviet women, Valentina Tereshkova and Svetlana Savitskaya, had been in space in 1963 and 1982 respectively.) She was Sally Ride.

Unlike many previous astronauts who had dreamed of being pilots since their childhood, Sally Ride never considered becoming an astronaut until she saw a NASA advertisement for astronauts in a school newspaper.

Sally K. Ride was born in Encino, California, on May 26, 1951. When she was a girl, her main interest was sports. A natural athlete, she often played baseball with boys in sandlots. She also loved the rough and tumble of football. An extraordinary tennis player, she was coached by Alice Marble, a four-time U.S. Open champion. Ride at one point ranked eighteenth nationally. She once played with Billie

Sally K. Ride, the first American woman astronaut.

Jean King, who tried to talk her into going professional. Thanks to her tennis skills, Ride was given a scholarship to Westlake School for Girls, a private prep school in Los Angeles.

Ride seemed headed for a career in tennis, but all that changed when she took a course in physiology. Ride loved the logical manner in which science was taught. She realized that by using science she could understand the world around her. Most of all, science appealed to her imagination.

Sally Ride eventually went to Stanford University, to Swarthmore College in Pennsylvania, and back to Stanford.

She graduated with two degrees, a B.A. in English and a B.S. in physics. In graduate school at Stanford, she studied X-ray astronomy and did advanced work on free electron lasers. She studied how electrons give off light when they are bent in a magnetic field. Although she did not know it at the time, NASA was deeply interested in this same subject.

Just before she received her doctorate in physics, Ride happened to see an ad for astronauts in a student newspaper. She was surprised, for she had had no idea that NASA ever advertised for astronauts. However, she answered the ad—so did 8,370 other applicants—and was chosen. Few of the others were.

To train as an astronaut, Ride learned to parachute, to survive at sea (in case a space shuttle landed on the waves), to think fast, and to fly jet airplanes.

Eventually she was given the demanding and difficult job of being a mission specialist. She was in charge of operating a mechanical arm, used somewhat like a crane, to launch and pick up satellites from the space shuttle.

On June 18, 1983, Ride went aloft in the space shuttle, *Challenger*, cheered on by a contingent of notable American women and by launch-watchers wearing T-shirts that read "Ride, Sally Ride." On her first day in space, Ride and Air Force Lieutenant Colonel John M. Fabian launched a Canadian communications satellite called *Anik-C*. The next day they launched an Indonesian satellite, called *Palapa B*, which would provide more than a million people in Southeast Asia with telephone service. Ride also did experiments to see how certain types of metals could be alloyed while in a weightless state. Ride's most important mission was to capture a satellite out in space, using the mechanical arm. She caught the *Shuttle Pallet* Satellite, repaired it, and placed it in orbit again. Later Ride again captured it and let it go, and then repeated the procedure several times. The satellite was finally placed in the cargo bay and brought back to Earth. NASA declared the project an unqualified success, their highest rating.

After an American woman had flown in space, many wondered when the first black American would go aloft. Hardly two months had passed when people no longer had to wonder. On August 30, 1983, Air Force Lieutenant Colonel Guion S. Bluford headed for space.

Guion Bluford, The First Black American in Space

Guion Bluford was born in Philadelphia, Pennsylvania, on November 22, 1942. His father was a mechanical engineer and inventor, and his mother was a schoolteacher.

Guion S. Bluford, the first black American astronaut.

Bluford was in many ways a typical American boy. He joined the Boy Scouts, sold newspapers to make extra money, and became fascinated with airplanes. In high school, he decided he would become an aerospace engineer. He loved mathematics and science and was a good student.

After graduating from Overbrook High School, Bluford enrolled in the aerospace engineering program at Pennsylvania State University. After college, he trained as a pilot at Williams Air Force Base in Arizona, receiving his wings in 1965. In 1967 he went to Vietnam. There he flew 144 combat missions, 65 of which took him over enemy territory in North Vietnam. He was awarded many decorations, including ten Air Force Air Medals.

In August 1972, he started graduate studies at the Air Force Institute of Technology at Wright-Patterson Air Force Base in Ohio, the leading Air Force engineering school. There he obtained an M.S. degree with distinction.

In January 1978, along with 8,370 other people, Bluford applied to become an astronaut. NASA chose only 35, among them Bluford and Sally Ride. In the same year, Bluford received his Ph.D. in aerospace engineering, with a minor in laser physics, from the Air Force Institute of Technology.

At 2:32 A.M. on August 30, 1983, the space shuttle *Challenger* rose above the launchpad. Of all the lift-offs ever seen at the Cape, this was perhaps the most spectacular. The flames and clouds of smoke and steam lit up the night sky so brightly that people in Miami—250 miles to the south—could see them.

Mission specialist Bluford worked on several projects. He helped launch one of the most interesting satellites ever put into orbit, the *Insat-1B*, belonging to the government of India. Its purpose was to help educate the hundreds of millions of Indians who live in small villages throughout the country. Television programs would relay lessons to them via the satellite. In addition to being an extraordinary educational tool, it would also help the Indian government predict dangerous storms.

Bluford also conducted medical experiments along with astronaut and mission specialist Dale Gardner and helped flight commander Richard Truly and pilot Dan Brandenstein during lift-off and landing.

With the completion of these successful missions, a new era of equality had begun. But statements by Sally Ride and Guion Bluford both revealed that it was not so much for reasons of sexual and racial equality that they found their space voyages wonderful, but because space, science, and adventure were their main concerns. Daring the unknown was both the challenge and the job at hand.

By 1983 the space shuttles were proving successful from a scientific point of view. Although problems remained and critics continued to cite the tremendous cost and the frequent delays, no one could argue with the space shuttle's marvelous safety record. In fact, in general NASA had an amazing record. Not a single American fatality had

Astronaut Bruce McCandless II on his historic extra-vehicular activity. He controls small nitrogen-propelled rockets with a device called the manned maneuvering unit (MMU), which he holds in his hand. The MMU allowed spacewalkers to move all alone for the first time—without lifelines—hundreds of feet away from the space shuttle orbiting the earth.

occurred in space. Indeed, no astronaut had become seriously ill in space nor been hurt in an accident. Even so, the 1967 deaths of Grissom, White, and Chaffee in a fire on the ground served to remind NASA of the ever-present risks of the space program.

THE FIRST CIVILIAN IN SPACE

On January 28, 1986, the space shuttle *Challenger* stood proudly on the launchpad, ready to go into orbit. It was a flight that NASA, and Americans everywhere, had looked forward to with a sense of joy and excitement.

For the first time in NASA's history a civilian—an ordinary person—would go into space. In a real sense the Space Age had arrived—not just for daring, highly trained astronauts, but for everybody.

On board was a 37-year-old schoolteacher from Concord, New Hampshire; her name was Christa McAuliffe. An excellent choice for the first ordinary person in space, she came from a background that lacked wealth and special advantages, and in television interviews she proved to be intelligent, cheerful, good-natured, and very excited about space.

Christa McAuliffe

Christa McAuliffe was born in Boston, Massachusetts, and named Sharon Christa Corrigan. Always active and on the go, she played softball, was a Girl Scout, sang with groups, played the piano, and took dance lessons. She went to a Framingham, Massachusetts, Roman Catholic high school and was a member of the National Honor Society. While in high school, she met her future husband, Steven McAuliffe. She also began to consider the vast possibilities connected with space. It fascinated her to imagine that someday people would live in space colonies.

After graduating from high school, she went to Framingham State College in Massachusetts, working on an

NASA's Teacher in Space, Christa McAuliffe, talking to reporters.

assembly line in order to put herself through school. Following graduation, she married Steven McAuliffe and went to Bowie College in Maryland for her masters degree in education. While Steven McAuliffe attended law school, Christa McAuliffe taught history in public schools in Maryland.

Active as ever, McAuliffe led a Girl Scout troop, raised money for a hospital, and worked in a day-care center. She also had two children, Scott and Caroline.

The family moved back to New England and eventually settled in Concord, a city of about 30,000 people located in southern New Hampshire. There she taught history in high school. She was a very imaginative teacher who continued to think up new and more interesting ways of teaching her students about the past as well as the present. She also taught economics and law. And when she had the time, she thought of space.

When President Reagan announced in August 1984

155

that he wanted to send a teacher into space as the first civilian passenger on the shuttle, Christa McAuliffe obtained an application and filled out each of its fifteen pages. So did 11,000 other American teachers.

NASA chose McAuliffe for many reasons. She was a typical teacher, never at a loss for an answer. Everyone loved her smile and marvelous laugh. She could speak easily about complex subjects and was always at ease. And she was very enthusiastic. Someday, she was convinced, people would live in space stations and in colonies on distant planets. Once she said that since she worked with students she touched the future. And for her the future meant new space frontiers.

When she was finally chosen, she wept with joy. She called her forthcoming voyage into space the ultimate field trip.

Like the toughest astronauts, McAuliffe had to undergo rigorous training. She had to learn survival techniques, and to experience weightlessness inside an airplane that would suddenly plummet to make her float. (She jokingly called the airplane the "vomit comet.")

Like other astronauts, she knew of the potential dangers in space and fully realized that it was possible for her to be killed in the space shuttle. Nothing in life, she knew, was risk-free. Yet she wanted to go aloft anyway. It was her goal to demystify space, she said, and especially to show children that space was in their future.

NASA was pleased with McAuliffe's excellence as a schoolteacher. While on board the *Challenger*, it was planned that she would hold televised classes in space for children all over America. Her lessons would be sent to ground-based television sets in tens of thousands of schools. NASA wanted children to know more about space, to understand it better. Her first lesson in space was to be about the safety features of the space shuttle, and the next was to be about why people would someday live and work in space. She intended to stress the human dimension, to explain to her students down on the ground over a hundred miles below her why space would change their lives.

A very experienced crew was to go up in the space shuttle *Challenger* along with McAuliffe.

Francis R. Scobee, a civilian, was commander. He had extensive experience as a test pilot. He had been the pilot on the *Challenger* in 1984 and was familiar with the spacecraft.

U.S. Navy Commander Michael J. Smith was the pilot. Though the trip would be his first in a space shuttle, he had flown 4,300 hours in various types of aircraft, mainly jets. He held the Navy Distinguished Flying Cross and three Air Medals, as well as others.

Dr. Ronald E. McNair, a physicist, was the crew member who was to launch a science platform to observe Halley's comet. He was the second black American to fly in space.

Air Force Lieutenant Colonel Ellison S. Onizuka was a mission specialist. He had been in space before on the space shuttle *Discovery*.

Dr. Judith A. Resnik was also a mission specialist. A member of the space shuttle *Discovery* crew, she was the second American woman to have been in space.

Gregory B. Jarvis, a civilian, was a Hughes Aircraft Company engineer who had never been in space before. His title was payload specialist. He would perform experiments on the way liquids behaved in a weightless condition.

DISASTER IN SPACE

The launch took place on a cold day—very cold for Florida. A large crowd of onlookers shivered in the frigid wind that blew at Cape Canaveral.

McAuliffe's students, who were gathered in her school

in Concord, New Hampshire, blew horns as the countdown was given—10, 9, 8, 7, 6, 5, 4, 3, 2, 1. They released balloons. Lift-off.

The huge engines roared. The ground trembled. The rocket shivered and began to move upward toward the endless sky. Everything looked perfect. Television cameras followed the rising rocket with the *Challenger* attached.

Then, on camera, millions of Americans saw a flame coming sideways out of the right rocket booster. The flame seemed to dance up and down along the side of the booster rocket.

Mission Control talked to Commander Scobee, who was at the controls of *Challenger*. "Challenger, go at throttle up."

Scobee answered, "Roger, go at throttle up."

Mission Control said, "We're at a minute 15 seconds, velocity 2,900 feet per second [1,977 miles per hour], altitude nine nautical miles [10.35 statute miles], range distance seven nautical miles [8.05 statute miles]."

Then there was a long silence.

People watching the lift-off at Cape Canaveral and millions more watching on television sets all over the world saw a sudden burst of flame. An enormous fireball from a huge explosion filled the Florida sky.

At first, the schoolchildren in McAuliffe's class in New Hampshire did not appear to understand what had happened. They laughed, released more balloons, and blew tin horns. A teacher, realizing something had gone wrong, told the cheering, laughing children to be quiet. One by one, it dawned on the students that a terrible accident had occurred in space and that their own teacher was up there.

The *Challenger* and the rockets exploded. All seven people aboard were killed.

The world was numb with shock. Americans and Russians cried in the streets. It was by far the worst space disaster ever.

President Ronald Reagan gave a sober and moving televised speech in which he told the nation that the space program would continue. He spoke of Francis Scobee, Mike Smith, Ronald E. McNair, Ellison S. Onizuka, Judith Resnik, and Gregory Jarvis. He spoke of Christa McAuliffe and of American schoolchildren of all ages. The world mourned the loss of the seven brave people who had been on board.

AFTER THE *CHALLENGER* DISASTER

NASA and the space program, already subjected to increasing criticism since the spectacular successes of the 1960s, were brought to a near standstill by the staggering failure of the space shuttle *Challenger*.

Months of inquiry revealed several causes of the disaster. Part of the responsibility lay in imperfections in NASA's organization. This problem showed up just before the disaster, when a warning to high officials about the dangers of launching in cold weather did not reach them. Information did not flow properly. But more basic was the problem of defective seals in the solid rockets. In the cold weather, they did not operate correctly, and hot gases leaked through them, burning a hole in the huge booster rocket. The heated fuel and liquid oxygen in it exploded.

Although steps were taken immediately following the disaster to correct the problems, the space shuttle program was in jeopardy. The president and his advisers, along with key congressional leaders and NASA officials, met repeatedly to discuss the future of the shuttle—and the future of the National Aeronautics and Space Administration. After lengthy discussions, President Reagan came to a decision in August 1986.

The *Challenger* would be replaced by a new space shuttle to be built over seven years at a cost between $2 and $3 billion, bringing back to four the total number of shuttles. Most of the money to pay for the new shuttle would come from funds saved by stopping any further shuttle programs for two years, and from cutbacks in other scheduled NASA programs; some would come from Congress. Shuttle flights would operate on a more limited basis and carry fewer astronauts. The president required that NASA get out of commercial business; no longer would it take up satellites and experiments for private industry and foreign countries. It would stick to military, scientific, and exploration activities. A separate private space industry would be greatly encouraged to take over some of NASA's programs. The U.S. government would subsidize the development of private launching vehicles and provide access to government launchpads at reduced rates.

Not many were pleased with the president's decision. Some felt that to build a new shuttle when three others were already available was a waste of money. Moreover, they considered it a continuation of a failed policy.

Others had the opposite complaint—that the space shuttle was the key to any future space program and needed more, not less, funding. Private companies, rather than welcoming the chance to develop their own launching capabilities, felt boxed in. No commercial company in America (or anyplace else) approaches the capabilities of NASA; it will take private enterprise years, even decades, to achieve them, and will cost billions of dollars. In the meantime, they have no alternative but to turn to the space programs of other countries—paying France, Japan, or even China or the Soviet Union to send up their satellites and conduct their research.

Finally, many have charged, the new policy will hand leadership of America's space program over to the Air Force. While severe cutbacks reduced funding for NASA and hundreds of other domestic programs during the mid-1980s, the president and Congress increased the military budget. Now the Department of Defense intends to develop a new orbiter, and the Air Force has announced plans to buy medium-sized rockets; to send up commercial satellites and other commercial payloads that the space shuttle formerly carried; and to build its own medium-sized rockets, yet to be designed.

Where these developments leave NASA remains to be seen. For the immediate future, most of its budget and energies will be spent on developing the new shuttle and making improvements in the three existing shuttles. What happens next will depend for the most part on the economy and on the degree of presidential, congressional, and public favor for NASA and for space exploration.

13

NASA's Future Plans

As the history of the American space program shows, American efforts in space have *always* been in response to current technology, American politics, public taste, and worldwide activities. It was not accidental that the Space Age coincided with the invention and development of computers, lasers, and powerful electronic equipment. The moon race was part of a political effort in America's foreign policy. *Sputnik* and other Russian space challenges spurred the creation of NASA and especially America's race to the moon. We cannot think of the future of any American space program without considering the world at large.

THE SPACE SHUTTLES OF THE FUTURE

France, China, the Soviet Union, and Japan are considering the design, manufacture, and use of space shuttles. Because these countries are moving ahead with their space shuttle programs, the United States is under pressure to keep its own space shuttle alive. In response, America has decided, at the very least, to replace the *Challenger* and to forge ahead with the space shuttle program. Already a space shuttle flight has been scheduled for early 1988, with a new crew named to go aboard the new shuttle, *Discovery*. Meanwhile, NASA's space shuttle *Atlantis* stands on a launchpad at Cape Canaveral, where among other rigorous tests, astronauts are practicing emergency escape exercises and NASA is making checks on the booster rockets.

In an important shift, the space agency is planning to devote most space shuttles to military missions, and NASA will give secret military satellite missions priority.

This new emphasis on the military began with an agreement reached in the early days of the shuttle program and has been gaining momentum for several years. A civilian government agency such as NASA can be ordered to carry out military missions if they are deemed necessary for national security. And that is what has been taking place. NASA will continue to devote more effort toward military missions, because of defense needs and because a backlog of military satellites await a launch.

The grounding of the shuttles following the *Challenger* disaster has put pressure on NASA to plan more military missions, seen by the president "as crucial to national security." Of the next missions planned by NASA, most are military. They are:

In the future, will such airplanes as this replace the space shuttles? This artist's conception shows an aerospace airplane that will be able to cruise in the atmosphere of the earth like an ordinary airplane—and to move out of the atmosphere and orbit the world as a spacecraft.

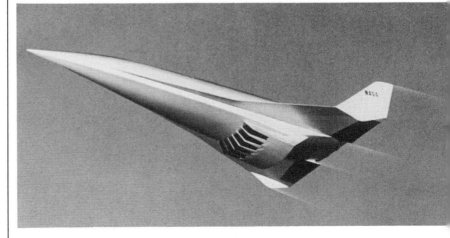

1. A tracking and relay satellite, listed as a military payload
2. A secret Pentagon mission
3. The deployment of either the *Galileo* or *Ulysses* planetary probe
4. A military mission, with a shuttle launch at Vandenberg Air Force Base in California
5. A launch of NASA's $1 billion space telescope
6. A Defense Department satellite
7. A tracking and relaying satellite
8. A mission for the proposed antimissile shield

It is clear that the space shuttles are at the heart of all NASA programs for the next few years. In fact, the next two years or more in space will be primarily devoted to space shuttle flights. This may hold true for many years, because NASA does not have a strong unmanned satellite or rocket program.

FUTURE EXPLORATION

Not all the work of NASA will be military. NASA still plans to send aloft a powerful optical telescope. This space telescope, which has already been manufactured, is merely waiting its turn on a space shuttle schedule. Unimpeded by the earth's wavering hundred-mile-thick atmosphere, it will "look" much farther out into space than any land-based telescope has. Once in space, it will provide us with a much clearer and far steadier view of distant stars.

In addition, NASA is planning another type of telescope—this one a radio telescope that should be in operation in the 1990s. In the autumn of 1986, a space radio telescope, called the TDRS (Tracking and Data Relay Satellite System) was used in conjunction with other ground-based telescopes located in White Sands, New Mexico, in Tidbinbilla, Australia, and in Usuda, Japan, to give astronomers radio images of distant stars that were sharper than anything previously obtained. The combined telescopes span a distance equal to 1.4 Earth diameters. In effect, the system operates as a gigantic telescope.

Using knowledge gained from the 1986 success with TDRS, NASA and the European Space Agency are planning to put into orbit an observatory called Quasat in the 1990s. Such a telescope will, it is believed, answer some deep space mysteries, especially about quasars billions of light-years away.

A SPACE STATION FOR THE 1990s

In September 1986, NASA administrator James C. Fletcher met with the House of Representatives Subcommittee on Space Science and Applications to unveil plans for a new space station design and assembly. The space station, consisting of five modules, will be built piece by piece while in a space orbit, beginning in 1993. A crew of from six to eight men and women will periodically use it for weeks or months at a time.

All the materials and men and women who will work on the space station will arrive at the orbiting construction site by way of space shuttles. Eight space shuttle flights per year are called for. (Originally, 16 a year were planned, but eight gives NASA a far better safety margin.) The design makes it possible for most construction work to be done inside rather than outside the space station, and for it to be built with fewer space shuttle trips.

The United States is not alone in its interest in building a space station. Europe, Canada, and Japan are likely to join in to make it an international project. In recent years, European countries, especially France, have made great strides in their space endeavors. The magazine *Aviation and Space Technology* pointed out that ESA, the European Space Agency, has become equal to NASA, and that ESA could even make and maintain a space station without NASA's help if it should want to.

On November 21, 1986, NASA and ESA officials met in Washington, D.C., to discuss international cooperation about sharing costs and responsibilities for the space shuttle. Out of that meeting came several proposals and indications of what we are likely to see in the future.

NASA seeks to have 80 percent of the responsibility for the space station operation, with ESA responsible for 15 percent and Canada and Japan responsible for the remainder. Japan plans to contribute a laboratory module to the proposed space station. Both NASA and ESA officials are optimistic that details of the agreement will be ironed out and the joint venture will soon come to fruition.

This international space station is very important. What happens now could shape the course of international efforts into the twenty-first century. Space exploration is rapidly becoming more and more of a worldwide concern, relying on the advanced technologies of many countries.

In the not-too-distant future, perhaps during our lifetime, we may see space stations permanently orbiting the earth. They would house astronauts, scientists, professional people, workers, and robots. They would contain factories, repair stations, offices, living quarters, and entertainment centers. Some people could live in space stations for years, perhaps for their whole lives. Shown here is but one of many designs being considered for a space station of the future.

THE GEOSPHERE-BIOSPHERE PROGRAM

Another cooperative effort involves atmospheric and ecological studies. In 1957–1958, countries all over the world participated in the "International Geophysical Year of 1957–1958." Thanks to the efforts of scientists from many countries working at sea, in far-off mountains, and especially in the Antarctic, our knowledge of the earth greatly expanded. The ocean floors were mapped, the Antarctic was explored in detail, and the theory of drifting continents was developed.

In the early 1990s there will be a similar undertaking, the "Geosphere-Biosphere Program: A Study of Global Change," planned by scientific academies of the United States, the Soviet Union, China, and other countries. The chairman of the American committee, Dr. John Eddy, went to Bern, Switzerland, in September 1986 to approve research for what will eventually be the "largest scientific program ever mounted."

Relying heavily on satellites and computers, the program will examine the increasing amount of carbon dioxide in the atmosphere and the higher temperatures that result. It will also study the intensive clearing of forests for agriculture. It will look at the many new chemicals that industries and cities release into the atmosphere, soil, and oceans. Acid rain, expanding deserts, the composition of soils and water, the diversity of plant and animal species, and the balance of life of the global ecosystem will all be studied.

INTO THE 21ST CENTURY

NASA's tentative long-range plans emerged from a presidential panel convened in early 1986. On May 22, 1986, Thomas O. Paine, who had been the administrator of NASA during the Apollo program, announced the results of the panel discussions. There will be new generations of space vehicles, he said—new types of rockets, space shuttles, and perhaps airplanes that can actually fly into space. New types of satellites and other equipment will be developed. Exotic, high-technology plans for much of this are on the drawing boards.

Paine also spoke of NASA's plans for future moon and Mars colonies. NASA expects to return to the moon in the year 2005. A colony of about 20 people might be established there to set up bases for mining, manufacturing, and scientific research. And in the year 2035, NASA could begin a colonization of Mars. According to the current administrator of NASA, James Fletcher, the panel's program is "a bold course of action for our nation . . . ambitious, yet achievable."

As *Scientific American* points out, the exploration of Mars should be the focus of the nation's space program. S. Fred Singer, a planetary scientist at the University of Virginia, states that the exploration of Mars will excite the popular imagination and focus NASA's programs for the next 10 to 20 years. And although no report actually spells it out, the establishment of a Martian base would be a long-awaited space triumph, particularly if life is discovered there.

Our knowledge—not only about space, but also of our own human biology and life itself—would be expanded into a new realm. Men and women would stay for months, if not years, on Mars—mainly because of its great distance from Earth. Spaceships would ferry passengers to and from Earth in regular six-month voyages, much like ocean liners travel across oceans. Human beings would truly be inhabitants of the solar system.

NASA, then, will continue to dare the unknown, to move outward into space, and to explore and colonize the planets and their moons. We stand at the edge of the great unknown. Marvelous space adventures we dream about are only years away. In a way, we are like the people of the late nineteenth century who dreamed of space travel. They would be led to the moon by Tsiolkovsky, Goddard, von Braun, and others. With NASA's guidance, we, too, will be taken on new travels to distant places in the heavens.

Bibliography

Armstrong, Neil; Michael Collins; Edwin E. Aldrin, Jr. *The First on the Moon*. Boston: Little, Brown, 1970. (This book, written by astronauts, is detailed and exciting.)

Collins, Michael. *Carrying the Fire*. New York: Farrar, Straus & Giroux, 1974. (Written by an astronaut who was on *Apollo 11*. The best inside view.)

Eddy, John A. *A New Sun: The Solar Result from Skylab*. Washington D.C.: NASA Sp-402, National Aeronautics and Space Administration, 1979. (This is the official NASA book describing Skylab. It is technical and difficult to read, but the pictures are excellent, and by browsing in the book one can experience the adventures of the astronauts in the world's first space station.)

Finnel, Richard O.; William Swindell; Eric Burgess. *Pioneer Odyssey*. Washington D.C.: NASA SP-376 National Aeronautics and Space Administration, 1977. (This official NASA book is highly technical and difficult to read. Yet a look at some of the text and the excellent pictures affords a good idea of all that goes into a planetary probe.)

Gardner, Robert. *Space: Frontiers of the Future*. New York: Doubleday, 1980. (This history of NASA is outdated but has interesting speculations on the future.)

The Illustrated Encyclopedia of Astronomy and Space. New York: Thomas Y. Crowell, 1976. (A good source book.)

Kerrod, Robin. *Space Shuttle.* New York: Gallery Books, 1984. (Adequate text. Many good pictures.)

Langston, John M. *The Decision to Go to the Moon.* Cambridge: MIT Press, 1970. (This is a thorough book about the politics of the moon race decision. A very difficult, scholarly book.)

Lewis, Richard S. *Appointment on the Moon.* New York: Viking Press, 1969. (A very thorough and interesting book.)

McDougall, Walter. *The Heavens and the Earth.* New York: Basic Books, 1985. (This Pulitzer prize-winning book takes a sharp look at the politics and sociological aspects of space.)

Mailer, Norman. *A Fire on the Moon.* Boston: Little, Brown, 1970. (A well-known author reflects on the human aspects of the moon flights.)

Ryan, Peter. *Solar System.* Foreword by Carl Sagan. New York: Viking Press, 1979. (One of the best books on the solar system, planets, and their moons.)

Sagan, Carl. *Cosmos.* New York: Random House, 1980. (An excellent book about astronomy and, to a lesser extent, space travel.)

Von Braun, Wernher, *Space Frontier.* New York: Holt, Rinehart & Winston, 1971. (This book, written by the world's expert rocket designer, is surprisingly easy to read and understand.)

Wilford, John Noble. *We Reach the Moon.* New York: New York Times Books, W. W. Norton, 1971. (A thorough book, not difficult to read and often exciting.)

Wolfe, Tom. *The Right Stuff.* New York: Farrar, Straus & Giroux, 1979.(An adult and at times difficult book from which the movie of the same title was made.)

Also consulted were issues of *Facts on File, National Geographic*, the *New York Review of Books*, the *New York Times*, *Scientific American*, and *Sky and Telescope*.

Index

173